Unity Animation Essentials

Bring your characters to life with the latest features of Unity and Mecanim

Alan Thorn

PUBLISHING

BIRMINGHAM - MUMBAI

Unity Animation Essentials

First published: June 2015

Production reference: 1180615

Published by Packt Publishing Ltd.
Livery Place
35 Livery Street
Birmingham B3 2PB, UK.

ISBN 978-1-78217-481-3

www.packtpub.com

Credits

Author
Alan Thorn

Reviewers
Adam Single
Bryan R. Venzen

Commissioning Editor
Nadeem N. Bagban

Acquisition Editor
Harsha Bharwani

Content Development Editor
Arwa Manasawala

Technical Editor
Madhunikita Sunil Chindarkar

Copy Editor
Vikrant Phadke

Project Coordinator
Shweta Birwatkar

Proofreader
Safis Editing

Indexer
Hemangini Bari

Production Coordinator
Shantanu N. Zagade

Cover Work
Shantanu N. Zagade

About the Author

Alan Thorn is a freelance game developer and author, with over 13 years of industry experience. He founded Wax Lyrical Games and is the creator of the award-winning game *Baron Wittard: Nemesis of Ragnarok*. He is also the author of over 10 video training courses and 15 books on game development, including *Mastering Unity Scripting*, *How to Cheat in Unity 5*, and *UDK Game Development*. Besides this, he is a visiting lecturer for the master's degree course in game design and development at the National Film and Television School, London.

Alan has worked as a freelancer on over 500 projects, including games, simulators, kiosks, serious games, and augmented-reality software for game studios, museums, and theme parks worldwide. He is currently working on two game projects. He also enjoys graphics, philosophy, yoga, and hiking. More information about him can be found at http://www.alanthorn.net.

About the Reviewers

Adam Single is a husband, father, professional developer, indie developer, lover of music, and gamer. He is a coder for 7bit Hero; a programmer in the tech team at Real Serious Games in Brisbane, Australia; a cofounder, programmer, and co-designer at Sly Budgie; and a co-organizer of the Game Technology Brisbane meetup.

Since entering the professional game development industry in 2011, he has worked on numerous mobile games, including the Android hit *Photon* and a preinstalled game for specific Disney Japan's handsets. Adam was a programmer in a team that created a huge interactive display at the Queensland University of Technology's amazing multitouch installation, which was named The Cube. This was done as part of Australia's first Digital Writing Residency. He has also worked on a team at Real Serious Games to create large-scale interactive simulations for mining and construction industries, some of which are virtual reality-based solutions using Oculus Rift. All of this has been done using the Unity game engine.

Adam has a passion for unique and engaging possibilities inherent in modern technology. When he's not working on exciting new game mechanics for Sly Budgie, he experiments with homemade VR using mobile phone technology, building mobile applications by utilizing modern web development techniques and pushing the exciting ideas behind 7Bit Hero's live music/multiplayer game interaction down whichever fascinating path it should happen to go down.

Bryan R. Venzen is a visual effects artist and animator from Tampa, Florida. Since graduating from Florida Interactive Entertainment Academy (FIEA) in 2011, he has been involved in VFX and animation for mobile, PC, and console game titles. Because of his skill set and experience in leadership, he is able to contribute to projects in a number of ways, including creating VFX for a number of production elements, working on NVIDIA's physics engine (PhysX), animating and modeling in packages such as Autodesk 3ds Max and Maya, level building on platforms and engines such as Unity and UDK, and actively participating in design discussions to improve overall production quality. Bryan is a quick learner and a self-motivated team player, proficient in a range of 3D packages, game engines, and tools. He is skilled in troubleshooting problems and works well in a fast-paced work environment. Creating entertaining content is his passion.

www.PacktPub.com

Support files, eBooks, discount offers, and more

For support files and downloads related to your book, please visit www.PacktPub.com.

Did you know that Packt offers eBook versions of every book published, with PDF and ePub files available? You can upgrade to the eBook version at www.PacktPub.com and as a print book customer, you are entitled to a discount on the eBook copy. Get in touch with us at service@packtpub.com for more details.

At www.PacktPub.com, you can also read a collection of free technical articles, sign up for a range of free newsletters and receive exclusive discounts and offers on Packt books and eBooks.

https://www2.packtpub.com/books/subscription/packtlib

Do you need instant solutions to your IT questions? PacktLib is Packt's online digital book library. Here, you can search, access, and read Packt's entire library of books.

Why subscribe?
- Fully searchable across every book published by Packt
- Copy and paste, print, and bookmark content
- On demand and accessible via a web browser

Free access for Packt account holders

If you have an account with Packt at www.PacktPub.com, you can use this to access PacktLib today and view 9 entirely free books. Simply use your login credentials for immediate access.

Table of Contents

Preface

There's no getting around it! Animation plays a crucial role almost everywhere in games, from a simple scenario, such as a moving spaceship, to a complex scenario, such as facial animation. You simply cannot build a complete game and a truly interactive experience without some degree of animation. In this book, we'll take a step-by-step journey through the extensive feature set offered by Unity for creating real-time animations. We'll approach the subject from the ground up. This book assumes no prior knowledge about animation or experience in animation in Unity. However, it does assume basic familiarity with the Unity engine in terms of level design, basic interface usage, and some fundamental knowledge of C# coding. Using only this as the starting point, it proceeds to break down the bewildering range of animation features and considers their application in real-world scenarios, helping you achieve tangible results quickly and easily. Now, let's see what's ahead of us...

What this book covers

Chapter 1, Animation Fundamentals, begins by considering animation formally as a concept — animation at its core. From there, this chapter considers miscellaneous and very practical cases of animation in Unity that specifically involve scripting. This includes working with deltaTime and animation curves and even animating Mesh UVs. Overall, this chapter marks the beginning of our journey through animation and features everything you need to know to move ahead.

Chapter 2, Sprite Animation, explores the world of 2D animation, examining the sprite feature set used to create 2D games, flip-book textures, and planar animation. We consider the Unity Sprite editor, animation frames, frame rates, and how to fix common problems.

Chapter 3, Native Animation, enables us to see animation more generally in Unity, for both 2D and 3D, using both the **Animation** window and Particle Systems. We look at two very practical and useful projects. First, we create a camera fly-through across a level. Then, we create a dust/firefly particle system, which is very commonly found in fantasy games.

Chapter 4, Noncharacter Animation with Mecanim, teaches you about a flagship feature of Unity, namely Mecanim. Mecanim refers to a collection of features that together make advanced and smooth animations possible, especially for characters. In this chapter, we see the more unconventional uses of Mecanim as we animate doors and other interactive elements in our levels.

Chapter 5, Character Animation Fundamentals, begins with an analysis of rigged character animation. In this chapter, we see how to animate humanoid skeletons and characters for real-time animation. We also consider how to import rigged characters and configure them optimally, ready for animation.

Chapter 6, Advanced Character Animation, follows logically from the previous chapter. Here, we take an imported and configured character in Unity, and then we animate it as a player-controlled character. This character will support idle and forward movement, for both walking and running, as well as turning animations for moving left and right.

Chapter 7, Blend Shapes, IK, and Movie Textures, marks the end of this book. This chapter covers the following topics: Blend Shapes, used to create facial animations and other morph-like motions; inverse kinematics, used to accurately position a character's feet and hands in real time; and movie textures, used to play movie files as a texture projected onto a geometry.

What you need for this book

This book contains almost everything you need to follow along. Each chapter considers practical, real-world projects for animation, and includes companion files that can be downloaded and used. The only thing you need, apart from this book and your concentration, is a copy of the latest version of Unity; at the time of writing this book, it's Unity 5. The Unity 5 software is available for free as a personal edition, and it can be downloaded from the Unity website at https://unity3d.com/. In addition to Unity, if you want to create rigged character models and other animated 3D assets, you'll also need 3D modelling and animation software, such as 3ds Max, Maya, or Blender. Blender can be downloaded and used for free from http://www.blender.org/. However, this book considers only animation in terms of Unity.

Who this book is for

If you have a basic understanding of Unity and are looking to expand your knowledge further, seeking to learn more about real-time animation, then this book is for you. This book assumes that you've already used Unity to build simple levels and write basic scripts and you're looking for something more, that is, understanding more advanced animation concepts. Specifically, you may want to learn how features such as Mecanim can not only help you create believable animation, but also make your work simpler and more efficient.

Conventions

In this book, you will find a number of text styles that distinguish between different kinds of information. Here are some examples of these styles and an explanation of their meaning.

Code words in text, database table names, folder names, filenames, file extensions, pathnames, dummy URLs, user input, and Twitter handles are shown as follows: "By default, all new scripts are created with two functions, Start and Update."

A block of code is set as follows:

```
using UnityEngine;
using System.Collections;
public class MoviePlay : MonoBehaviour
{
  //Reference to movie to play
  public MovieTexture Movie = null;
  // Use this for initialization
  void Start ()
  {
    //Get Mesh Renderer Component
    MeshRenderer MeshR = GetComponent<MeshRenderer>();
    //Assign movie texture
    MeshR.material.mainTexture = Movie;
    GetComponent<AudioSource>().clip = Movie.audioClip;
    GetComponent<AudioSource>().spatialBlend=0;
    Movie.Play();
    GetComponent<AudioSource>().Play();
  }
}
```

When we wish to draw your attention to a particular part of a code block, the relevant lines or items are set in bold:

```
using UnityEngine;
using System.Collections;
public class Mover : MonoBehaviour
{
  // Use this for initialization
  void Start () {
  }
  // Update is called once per frame
  void Update ()
  {
    //Transform component on this object
    Transform ThisTransform = GetComponent<Transform>();
    //Add 1 to x axis position
    ThisTransform.position += new Vector3(1f,0f,0f);
  }
}
```

New terms and **important words** are shown in bold. Words that you see on the screen, for example, in menus or dialog boxes, appear in the text like this: "Once the curve is constructed, give the code a test run by playing the Unity project, and see the effect it has in the **Game** tab."

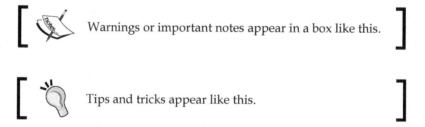

Warnings or important notes appear in a box like this.

Tips and tricks appear like this.

Reader feedback

Feedback from our readers is always welcome. Let us know what you think about this book—what you liked or disliked. Reader feedback is important for us as it helps us develop titles that you will really get the most out of.

To send us general feedback, simply e-mail feedback@packtpub.com, and mention the book's title in the subject of your message.

If there is a topic that you have expertise in and you are interested in either writing or contributing to a book, see our author guide at www.packtpub.com/authors.

Customer support

Now that you are the proud owner of a Packt book, we have a number of things to help you to get the most from your purchase.

Downloading the example code

You can download the example code files from your account at http://www. packtpub.com for all the Packt Publishing books you have purchased. If you purchased this book elsewhere, you can visit http://www.packtpub.com/support and register to have the files e-mailed directly to you.

Downloading the color images of this book

We also provide you with a PDF file that has color images of the screenshots/ diagrams used in this book. The color images will help you better understand the changes in the output. You can download this file from https://www.packtpub. com/sites/default/files/downloads/4813OT_ColoredImages.pdf.

Errata

Although we have taken every care to ensure the accuracy of our content, mistakes do happen. If you find a mistake in one of our books—maybe a mistake in the text or the code—we would be grateful if you could report this to us. By doing so, you can save other readers from frustration and help us improve subsequent versions of this book. If you find any errata, please report them by visiting http://www.packtpub. com/submit-errata, selecting your book, clicking on the **Errata Submission Form** link, and entering the details of your errata. Once your errata are verified, your submission will be accepted and the errata will be uploaded to our website or added to any list of existing errata under the Errata section of that title.

To view the previously submitted errata, go to https://www.packtpub.com/books/ content/support and enter the name of the book in the search field. The required information will appear under the **Errata** section.

Piracy

Piracy of copyrighted material on the Internet is an ongoing problem across all media. At Packt, we take the protection of our copyright and licenses very seriously. If you come across any illegal copies of our works in any form on the Internet, please provide us with the location address or website name immediately so that we can pursue a remedy.

Please contact us at copyright@packtpub.com with a link to the suspected pirated material.

We appreciate your help in protecting our authors and our ability to bring you valuable content.

Questions

If you have a problem with any aspect of this book, you can contact us at questions@packtpub.com, and we will do our best to address the problem.

1
Animation Fundamentals

Greetings and welcome to this journey through the animation feature set in the world of Unity. The importance of animation cannot be understated. Without animation, everything in-game would be statuesque, lifeless and perhaps boring. This holds true for nearly everything in games: doors must open, characters must move, foliage should sway with the wind, sparkles and particles should explode and shine, and so on. Consequently, learning animation and how to animate properly will unquestionably empower you as a developer, no matter what your career plans are. As a subject, animation creeps unavoidably into most game fields, and it's a critical concern for all members of a team—obviously for artists and animators, but also for programmers, sound designers, and level designers. This book is both valuable and relevant for most developers, and it aims to quickly and effectively introduce the fundamental concepts and practices surrounding animation in real-time games, specifically animation in Unity. By the end of this book, if you read each chapter carefully in order, you'll gain solid knowledge and a skill set in animation. You will be capable of making effective animations that express your artistic vision, as well as gaining an understanding of how and where you can expand your knowledge to the next level. But to reach that stage we'll begin here, in Chapter 1, with the most basic concepts of animation—the groundwork for any understanding of animation.

Understanding animation

At its most fundamental level, animation is about a relationship between two specific and separate properties, namely **change** on one hand and **time** on the other. Technically, animation defines change over time, that is, how a property adjusts or varies across time, such as how the position of a car changes over time, or how the color of a traffic light transitions over time from red to green. Thus, every animation occurs for a total length of time (**duration**), and throughout its lifetime, the properties of the objects will change at specific moments (**frames**), anywhere from the beginning to the end of the animation.

This definition is itself technical and somewhat dry, but relevant and important. However, it fails to properly encompass the aesthetic and artistic properties of animation. Through animation and through creative changes in properties over time, moods, atmospheres, worlds, and ideas can be conveyed effectively. Even so, the emotional and artistic power that comes from animation is ultimately a product of the underlying relationship of change with time. Within this framework of change over time, we may identify further key terms, specifically in computer animation. You may already be familiar with these concepts, but let's define them more formally.

Frames

Within an animation, *time* must necessarily be divided into separate and discrete units where change can occur. These units are called **frames**. Time is essentially a continuous and unbreakable quantity, insofar as you can always subdivide time (such as a second) to get an even smaller unit of time (such as a millisecond), and so on. In theory, this process of subdivision could essentially be carried on ad infinitum, resulting in smaller and smaller fractions of time. The concept of a **moment** or **event** in time is, by contrast, a human-made, discrete, and self-contained entity. It is a discrete thing that we perceive in time to make our experience of the world more intelligible. Unlike time, a moment is what it is, and it cannot be broken down into something smaller without ceasing to exist altogether. Inside a **moment**, or a **frame**, things can happen. A frame is an opportunity for properties to change—for doors to open, characters to move, colors to change, and more. In video game animation specifically, each second can sustain or contain a specified number of frames. The amount of frames passing within a second will vary from computer to computer, depending on the hardware capacity, the software installed, and other factors. The frame capacity per second is called **FPS (frames per second)**. It's often used as a measure of performance for a game, since lower frame rates are typically associated with jittery and poor performance. Consider the following figure, showing how frames divide time:

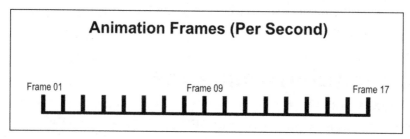

Frames divide time

Key frames

Although a frame represents an opportunity for change, it doesn't necessarily mean change *will* occur. Many frames can pass by in a second, and not every frame requires a change. Moreover, even if a change needs to happen for a frame, it would be tedious if animators had to define every frame of action. One of the benefits of computer animation, contrasted with manual, or "old", animation techniques, is that it can make our lives easier. Animators can instead define key, or important, frames within an animation sequence, and then have the computer automatically generate the intervening frames. Consider a simple animation in which a standard bedroom door opens by rotating outwards on its hinges by 90 degrees. The animation begins with the door in the closed position and ends in an open position. Here, we have defined two key states for the door (open and closed), and these states mark the beginning and end of the animation sequence. These are called **key frames**, because they define key moments within the animation. On the basis of key frames, Unity (as we'll see) can autogenerate the in-between frames (**tweens**), smoothly rotating the door from its starting frame to its ending frame. The mathematical process of generating tweens is termed as **interpolation**. See the following figure, showing how frames are generated between key frames:

Tweens are generated between key frames using interpolation

Animation types

The previous section defined the core concepts underpinning animation generally. Specifically, it covered change, time, frames, key frames, tweens, and interpolation. On the basis of this, we can identify several types of animation in video games from a technical perspective, as opposed to an artistic one. All variations depend on the concepts we've seen, but they do so in different and important ways. These animation types are significant for Unity because the differences in their nature require us to handle and work with them differently, using specific workflows and techniques that we will cover in the upcoming chapters. The animation types are listed throughout this section, as follows.

Rigid body animation

Rigid body animation is used to create pre-made animation sequences that move or change the properties of objects, considering those objects as whole or complete entities, as opposed to objects with smaller and moving parts. Some examples of this type of animation are a car racing along the road, a door opening on its hinges, a spaceship flying through space on its trajectory, and a piano falling from the side of a building. Despite the differences among these examples, they all have an important common ingredient. Specifically, although the object changes across key frames, it does so as a single and complete object. In other words, although the door may rotate on its hinges from a closed state to an open state, it still ends the animation as a door, with the same internal structure and composition as before. It doesn't morph into a tiger or a lion. It doesn't explode or turn into jelly. It doesn't melt into rain drops. Throughout the animation, the door retains its physical structure. It changes only in terms of its position, rotation and scale. Thus, in rigid body animation, changes across key frames apply to whole objects and their highest level properties. They do not filter down to subproperties and internal components, and they don't change the essence or internal forms of objects. These kinds of animation can be defined either directly in the Unity animation editor, as we'll see in later chapters, or inside 3D animation software (such as Maya, Max, or Blender) and then imported to Unity through mesh files. *Chapter 3, Native Animation*, covers rigid body animation further.

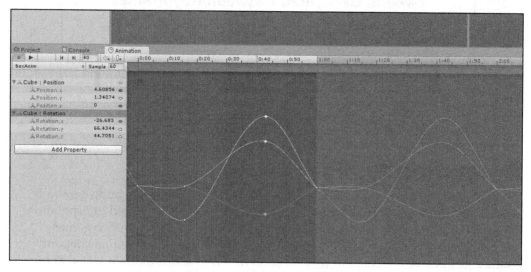

Key frame animation for rigid bodies

Rigged or bone-based animation

If you need to animate human characters, animals, flesh-eating goo, or exploding and deforming objects, then rigid body animation probably won't be enough. You'll need bone-based animation (also called rigged animation). This type of animation changes not the position, rotation, or scale of an object, but the movement and deformation of its internal parts across key frames. It works like this: the animation artist creates a network of special bone objects to approximate the underlying skeleton of a mesh, allowing independent and easy control of the surrounding and internal geometry. This is useful for animating arms, legs, head turns, mouth movements, tree rustling, and a lot more. Typically, bone-based animation is created as a complete animation sequence in 3D modeling software and is imported to Unity inside a mesh file, which can be processed and accessed via Mecanim, the Unity animation system. Chapters 5, 6, and 7 cover bone-based animation in greater detail.

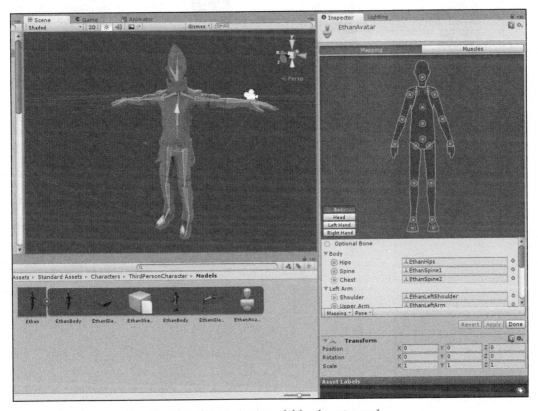

Bone-based animation is useful for character meshes

Sprite animation

For 2D games, graphical user interfaces, and a variety of special effects in 3D (such as water textures), you'll sometimes need a standard quad or plane mesh with a texture that animates. In this case, neither the object moves, as with rigid body animation, nor do any of its internal parts change, as with rigged animation. Rather, the texture itself animates. This animation type is called **sprite animation**. It takes a sequence of images or frames and plays them in order at a specified frame rate to achieve a consistent and animated look, for example, a walk cycle for a character in a 2D side-scrolling game. More information on sprite animation is given in the next chapter.

Sprite animation

Physics-based animation

In many cases, you can predefine your animation. That is, you can fully plan and create animation sequences for objects that will play in a predetermined way at runtime, such as walk cycles, sequences of door opening, explosions, and others. But sometimes, you need animation that appears realistic and yet responds to its world dynamically, based on decisions made by the player and other variable factors of the world that cannot be predicted ahead of time. There are different ways to handle these scenarios, but one is to use the Unity physics system, which includes components and other data that can be attached to objects to make them behave realistically. Examples of this include falling to the ground under the effects of gravity, and bending and twisting like cloth in the wind.

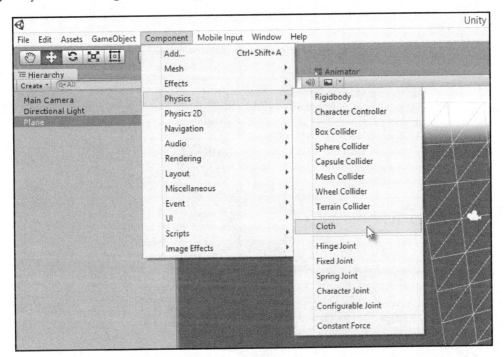

Physics animation

Morph animation

Occasionally, none of the animation methods you've read so far—rigid body, physics-based, rigged, or sprite animation—give you what's needed. Maybe, you need to morph one thing into another, such as a man into a werewolf, a toad into a princess, or a chocolate bar into a castle. In some instances, you need to blend, or merge smoothly, the state of a mesh in one frame into a different state in a different frame. This is called morph animation, or blend shapes. Essentially, this method relies on snapshots of a mesh's vertices across key frames in an animation, and blends between the states via tweens. The downside to this method is its computational expense. It's typically performance intensive, but its results can be impressive and highly realistic. We'll see blend shapes in detail later in *Chapter 7, Blend Shapes, IK, and Movie Textures*. See the following screenshot for the effects of blend shapes:

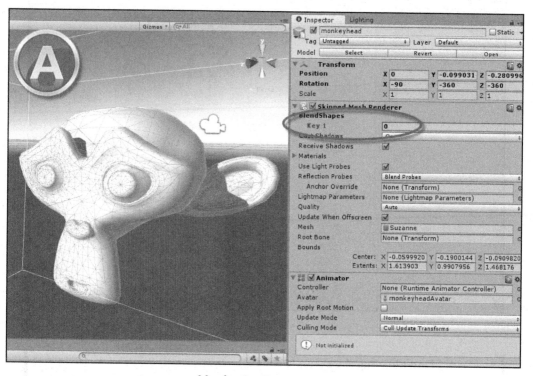

Morph animation start state

BlendShapes transition a model from one state to another. See the following figure for the destination state:

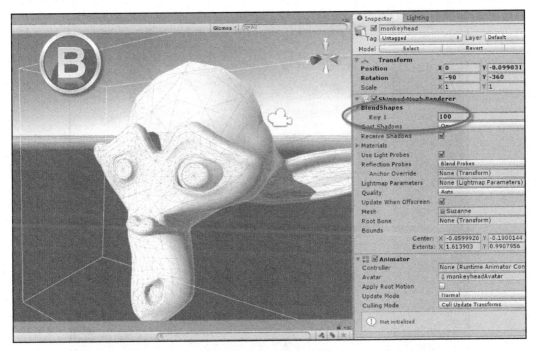

Morph animation end state

Video animation

Perhaps one of Unity's lesser known animation features is its ability to play video files as animated textures on desktop platforms and full-screen movies on mobile devices such as iOS and Android devices. Unity accepts OGV (Ogg Theora) videos as assets, and can replay both videos and sounds from these files as an animated texture on mesh objects in the scene. This allows developers to replay pre-rendered video file output from any animation package directly in their games.

This feature is powerful and useful, but also performance intensive. *Chapter 7, Blend Shapes, IK, and Movie Textures*, describes video animation in more depth.

Video file animation

Particle animation

Most animation methods considered so far are for clearly defined, tangible things in a scene, such as sprites and meshes. These are objects with clearly marked boundaries that separate them from other things. But you'll frequently need to animate less tangible, less solid, and less physical matter, such as smoke, fire, bubbles, sparkles, smog, swarms, fireworks, clouds, and others. For these purposes, a particle system is indispensable. As we'll see in *Chapter 3, Native Animation*, particle systems are entirely configurable objects that can be used to simulate rain, snow, flock of birds, and more. See the following screenshot for a particle system in action:

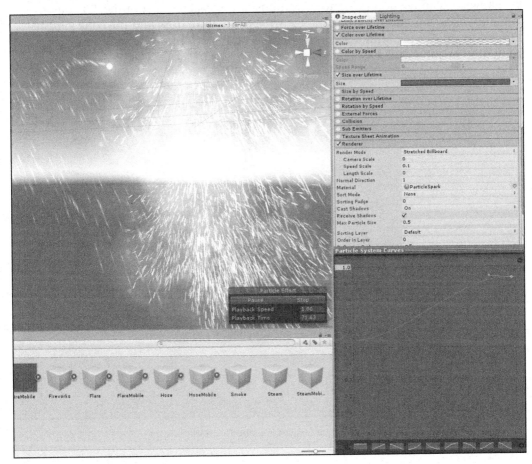

Particle system animation

Programmatic animation

Surprisingly, the most common animation type is perhaps programmatic animation, or dynamic animation. If you need a spaceship to fly across the screen, a user-controlled character to move around an environment, or a door to open when approached, you'll probably need some programmatic animation. This refers to changes made to properties in objects over time, which arise because of programming—code that a developer has written specifically for that purpose. Unlike many other forms of animation, the programmatic form is *not* created or built *in advance* by an artist or animator per se, because its permutations and combinations cannot be known upfront. So, it's coded by a programmer and has the flexibility to change and adjust according to conditions and variables at runtime. Of course, in many cases, animations are made by artists and animators and the code simply triggers or guides the animation at runtime. You'll learn more on programmatic animation in subsequent sections of this chapter.

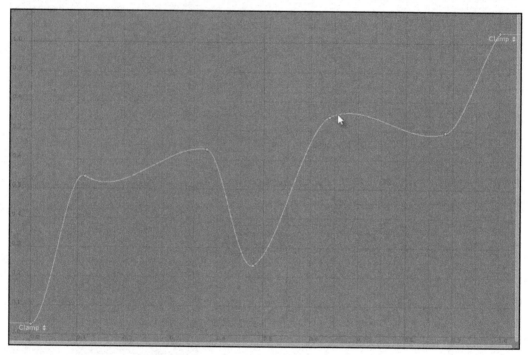

Programmatic animation is controlled through script

Animating through code – making things move

Animating through code is a great way to start animating generally, as it demonstrates all the core concepts we've seen so far, so let's try it. For this section, and the remaining sections, we'll use C# for scripting wherever applicable. However, since this book focuses on animation, I won't be explaining basic coding concepts here (such as variables, loops, and functions). Instead, I'll assume you already have basic to intermediate coding knowledge. If you want to learn coding, I recommend my 3dmotive video course *C# For Unity Developers* (available at http://3dmotive. com/) and *Learning C# by Developing Games with Unity 3D Beginner's Guide*, *Packt Publishing*.

By the end of the next few sections, we'll have created a game object (for example, a spaceship) that can travel at a constant speed in a single direction across the level. To get started, create a new script file by right-clicking inside the Project panel. Go to **Create | C# Script** from the context menu. Alternatively, go to **Assets | Create | C# Script** from the application menu, as shown in the following screenshot. Name the file Mover.cs. This script will be attached to any object that will move.

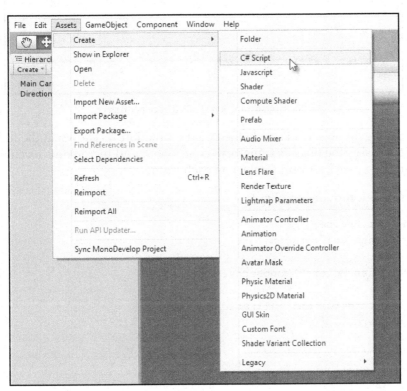

Now open the script file in MonoDevelop by double-clicking on it from the Project panel. By default, all new scripts are created with two functions: Start and Update. The Update function is of special significance for animation because it's related to frames and the frame rate. Specifically, it's called on every frame at runtime. This means that for a game with an FPS of 70, the Update function is called 70 times per second for each object with the script attached, provided the object is active. This makes Update important for animation because it gives us an opportunity to adjust an object's properties continually over time.

The Update function is called once per frame

To start moving an object, let's code the Update function, as shown in the following snippet. It accesses the object's **transform** component and increments its current position in the *x* axis by 1 unit (meter) on each frame.

Code sample 1-1: moving an object:

```
using UnityEngine;
using System.Collections;

public class Mover : MonoBehaviour
{
  // Use this for initialization
  void Start () {

  }
```

```
// Update is called once per frame
void Update ()
{
  //Transform component on this object
  Transform ThisTransform = GetComponent<Transform>();

  //Add 1 to x axis position
  ThisTransform.position += new Vector3(1f,0f,0f);
}
}
```

If you haven't already tested the code, drag and drop the script file onto an object in the scene. Then press the **Play** button. Depending on your view, the object may move too fast to be visible. Be sure to position your camera for a good view, and you should see your object spring to life by moving continually on the *x* axis.

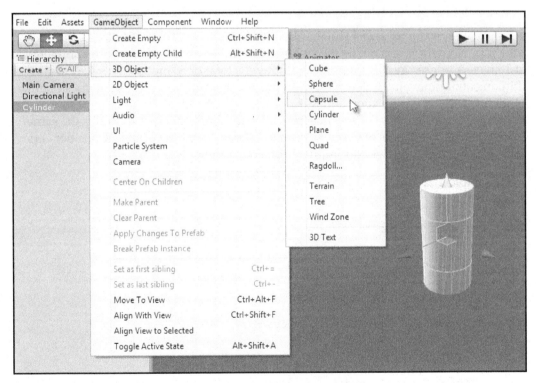

Adding the Mover script to an object in the scene

Consistent animation – speed, time, and deltaTime

The code in sample 1-1 works, but there's an important animation problem, and we should address it directly. As we've seen, the object travels along the *x* axis by 1 unit on every call to Update, that is, on each frame. This is potentially a problem because frame rates differ across computers, and even over time on the same computer. This means that different users will get different experiences while using our code because the object will move at varying speeds. Specifically, on a system with an FPS of 70, the object will be updated by 70 units every second. But on a different system running at 90 FPS, the object will move 90 units in the same time. This is bad, because we want all users to get a consistent in-game experience, experiencing time at the same speed and in the same way. This issue is especially important for multiplayer games, where it's critical that all users are in sync. To solve this issue, we need to approach the task differently, thinking in terms of speed and time.

To calculate how far an object should travel over time, we can use the speed-distance-time formula, where *distance traveled = speed x time*. This means that an object traveling at 10 meters per second for 5 seconds will travel a total of 50 meters. This way of thinking about movement doesn't rely on frame rates and frames. Also, it doesn't link motion to the Update function and its frequency specifically. Instead it maps motion to time directly, and time is consistent across all computers; that is, 1 second is the same everywhere. To code this in Unity, we can use the deltaTime variable. Consider code sample 1-2, which updates and improves on code sample 1-1.

Code sample 1-2: setting an object's speed:

```
using UnityEngine;
using System.Collections;

public class Mover : MonoBehaviour
{
  //Amount to travel (in metres) per second
  public float Speed = 1f;

  // Update is called once per frame
  void Update ()
  {
    //Transform component on this object
    Transform ThisTransform = GetComponent<Transform>();

    //Update X Axis position by 1 metre per second
    ThisTransform.position += new Vector3(Speed * Time.
deltaTime,0f,0f);
  }
}
```

The `deltaTime` variable is a native Unity variable updated every frame, and is part of the `Time` class. On each frame, it expresses (in seconds) how much time has elapsed since the previous frame. Therefore, if `deltaTime` is 0.5, then it means 1/2 of a second has elapsed since the previous frame, that is, since the `Update` function was last called. This is highly important information because, when multiplied by speed values, we always scale the speed value to be consistent with the frame rate for the current computer, ensuring a consistent speed across computers. By doing this, we make all speed values work the same for everybody. Now try this code in the editor and see the difference. Our objects will now move at the same speed on all computers.

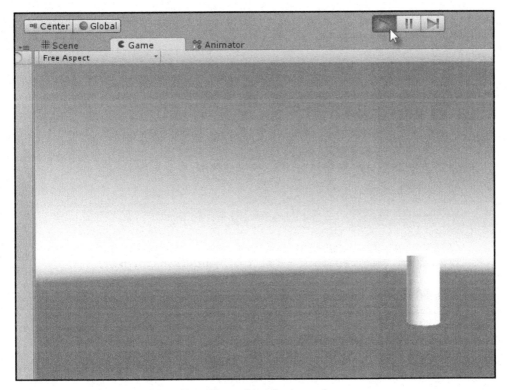

Press Play and test the new code

Movement in a direction

Based on code sample 1-2, we now have an object that moves in the x axis at a consistent speed. But how can the code be adapted to move in a different direction? If we wanted to move in only the y or z direction, we could've adapted the code easily. But what about movement in any arbitrary direction, including diagonals? For this, we need vectors. A vector is a three-component number in the form of (x, y, z), representing a direction. For example, $(0, 1, 0)$ means up (since the up-down axis is y) and $(0, 0, 1)$ means forward (since the z axis represents the forward-backward axis).

Code sample 1-3: controlling the direction:

```
using UnityEngine;
using System.Collections;

public class Mover : MonoBehaviour
{
  //Amount to travel (in metres) per second
  public float Speed = 1f;

  //Direction to travel
  public Vector3 Direction = Vector3.zero;

  // Update is called once per frame
  void Update ()
  {
    //Transform component on this object
    Transform ThisTransform = GetComponent<Transform>();

    //Update position in specified direction by speed
    ThisTransform.position += Direction.normalized * Speed * Time.
deltaTime;
  }
}
```

Now return to your object in the scene. The object inspector shows a `Direction` variable that can be edited to specify the direction in which the object should move. Movement along the *x* axis is due to (*1, 0, 0*) or (*-1, 0, 0*), and the numbers are similar for the other axes. You can also travel in diagonals using (*1, 1, 1*), which means moving in all three axes simultaneously.

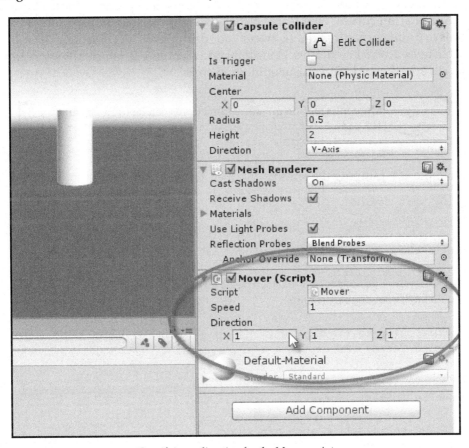

Specifying a direction for the Mover script

 The Unity project for this assignment can be found in this book's companion files in the `Chapter01/Moving Object` folder.

Coding tweens with animation curves

For objects that move continually at a constant speed and in a straight line, the code created in sample 1-3 works exactly as expected. But when animating, you'll typically want objects to move along curved paths, not just straight paths. Or you'd want objects to travel at variable speeds as opposed to constant speeds. To solve this, we can use **animation curves**, which are special objects (available only in Unity Pro) that allow us to build curves that define tweens for the animation, controlling how an object changes across key frames. Consider code sample 1-4, which allows us to vary an object's speed over time with an animation curve.

 More information on animation curves can be found online at `http://docs.unity3d.com/Manual/animeditor-AnimationCurves.html`.

Code sample 1-4: ramping the speed:

```
using UnityEngine;
using System.Collections;

public class Mover : MonoBehaviour
{
  //Maximum Speed to travel (in metres) per second
  public float Speed = 1f;

  //Direction to travel
  public Vector3 Direction = Vector3.zero;

  //Curve to adjust speed
  public AnimationCurve AnimCurve;

  // Update is called once per frame
  void Update ()
  {
    //Transform component on this object
    Transform ThisTransform = GetComponent<Transform>();

    //Update position in specified direction by speed
ThisTransform.position += Direction.normalized * Speed * AnimCurve.
Evaluate(Time.time) * Time.deltaTime;
  }
}
```

With the code in sample 1-4, select the animated object in the scene and examine the object inspector. The public `AnimCurve` variable is now visible as a graph.

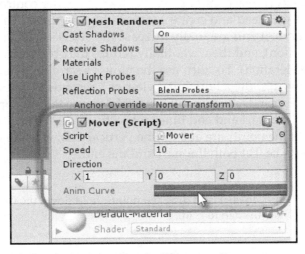

Accessing the animation curve editor

Click on the graph in the inspector to show the graph editor as a separate dialog. This graph allows you to control the tweens applied to the speed value. The horizontal axis represents time (in seconds), and the vertical axis represents the value (speed).

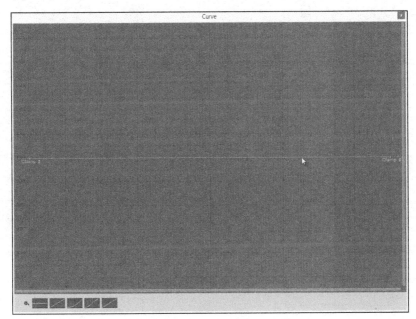

Building an animation curve

You can click any of the bottom-left curve presets to generate an initial curve, controlling interpolation for object speed. You can also double-click anywhere along the curve to insert new control points, allowing greater control of the curve's shape. Let's go ahead and create a famous type of curve in animation — an ease-in-ease-out curve. It will gradually increase the object's speed at the start of the animation (acceleration), and then eventually reduce the object's speed towards a complete stop (deceleration). To start, use the mouse's scrolling wheel to zoom out from the curve view, to show a horizontal view of 5 seconds in all from 0 seconds at animation start to 5 seconds at animation end. Make sure that the first and last key frame points rest at the start and end times respectively on the horizontal axis. Also make sure that both the points are at 0 for the vertical axis, which means that the object's speed should be 0 at both the start and the end.

[As you click and drag the points, hold down the *Ctrl* key to snap to grid.]

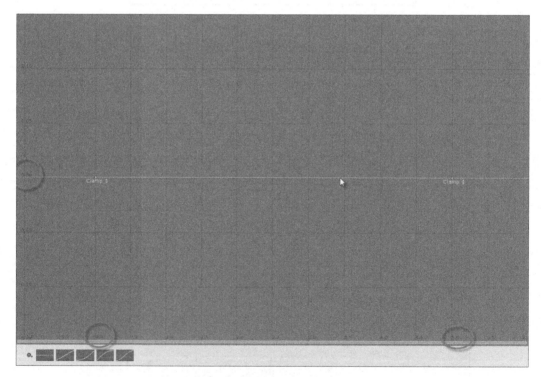

Starting an animation curve

To build an ease-in-ease-out curve, insert a new control point at the curve's center (at time equal to 2.5 seconds), and drag it upward on the vertical axis to a value of 1, representing the maximum speed for the object at that time. If the new control point forms a hard-edged angle in the curve, preventing it from being smooth, then right-click on the control point and select the **Free Smooth** option from the context menu to smooth out the curve.

[

You can press *F* to resize the graph view to get the curve fully in view.
]

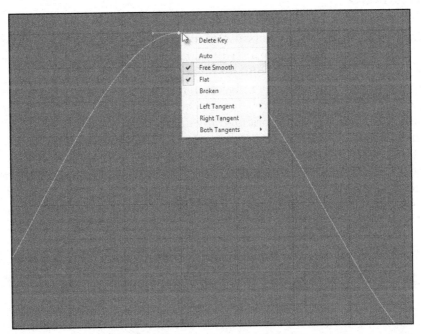

Creating an ease-in-ease-out curve for speed

Once the curve is constructed, give the code a test run by playing the Unity project, and see the effect it has in the **Game** tab. Based on code sample 1-4, the speed of the object will necessarily animate according to the curve over time. The AnimationCurve.Evaluate method accepts a time value as the input (on the horizontal axis) and returns an associated value from the *y* axis as a multiplier for speed. Using this function, we can evaluate any curve for programmatic animation.

More information on the Evaluate method can be found at the official Unity documentation at http://docs.unity3d.com/ScriptReference/AnimationCurve.html.

The Unity project for this assignment can be found in this book's companion files in the Chapter01/animation_curves folder.

Rotating towards objects – animation with coroutines

Now let's try a different programmatic animation scenario using **coroutines**, a special kind of function that are very useful for creating types of behavior that unfold over time. Specifically, we'll create a script that slowly and smoothly rotates an object to always face its target. This is useful for building enemies that always turn to look at you, rotating gun turrets, or other objects that must track a target. It should be emphasized here that the intended behavior isn't simply the LookAt behavior, which causes objects to immediately be oriented towards a target using the Transform.LookAt function. Instead, we're coding a kind of behavior in which an object always rotates at a specified angular speed to face a target, as shown in the following screenshot. The object may or may not be looking at its target at a particular moment, but it'll always be trying to look at it. This involves rotation and turning over time to look at its target, wherever the latter moves. Consider the code file (LookAt.cs) in sample 1-5.

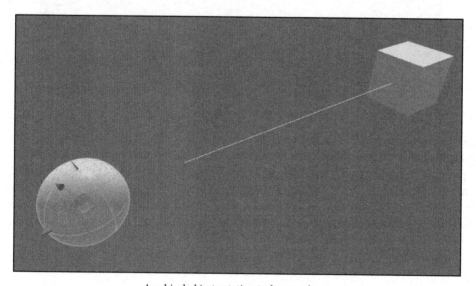

A cubical object rotating to face a sphere

More information on coroutines can be found in the Unity official documentation at `http://docs.unity3d.com/Manual/Coroutines.html`.

Code sample 1-5: rotating to face a target:

```
//-------------------------------------------
using UnityEngine;
using System.Collections;
[ExecuteInEditMode]
//-------------------------------------------
public class LookAt : MonoBehaviour
{
  //Cached transform
  private Transform ThisTransform = null;

  //Target to look at
  public Transform Target = null;

  //Rotate speed
  public float RotateSpeed = 100f;

  //-------------------------------------------
  // Use this for initialization
  void Awake () {
    //Get transform for this object
    ThisTransform = GetComponent<Transform>();
  }
  //-------------------------------------------
  void Start()
  {
    //Start tracking target
    StartCoroutine(TrackRotation(Target));
  }
  //-------------------------------------------
  //Coroutine for turning to face target
  IEnumerator TrackRotation(Transform Target)
  {
    //Loop forever and track target
    while(true)
    {
      if(ThisTransform != null && Target != null)
      {
        //Get direction to target
```

```
        Vector3 relativePos = Target.position -
          ThisTransform.position;

        //Calculate rotation to target
        Quaternion NewRotation = Quaternion.LookRotation(relativePos);

        //Rotate to target by speed
        ThisTransform.rotation =
          Quaternion.RotateTowards(ThisTransform.rotation,
          NewRotation, RotateSpeed * Time.deltaTime);
      }

    //wait for next frame
    yield return null;
    }
  }
  //----------------------------------------------
  //Function to draw look direction in viewport
  void OnDrawGizmos()
  {
    Gizmos.DrawLine(ThisTransform.position, ThisTransform.forward.
normalized * 5f);
  }
  //--------------------------------------------
}
//----------------------------------------------
```

Coroutines work differently from regular functions. They always feature an `IEnumerator` return type and contain at least one `yield` statement. Unlike regular functions, which perform their work line by line and then terminate, after which program execution resumes, coroutines seem to run in parallel with the process that invoked them. They feel and work much like a thread or background process — though without truly being so — multitasking and running alongside other processes. This makes them useful for animation, allowing us to animate and change properties for objects while other processes are running.

 The Unity project for this assignment can be found in this book's companion files in the `Chapter01/RotatingObjects` folder.

Material and mapping animation

Another really useful animation technique is UV or mapping animation, as shown in the following screenshot. This involves programmatically tweaking or changing the UV coordinates across a mesh's vertices over time to slide or move around the texture on its surface. This doesn't change or alter the pixels inside the texture itself, but rather animates where the pixels are mapped on the surface. Using UV animation, various effects can be created, such as animated water, flowing lava, moving clouds, warp tunnel effects, and lots more. Consider code sample 1-6 (`MatScroller.cs`).

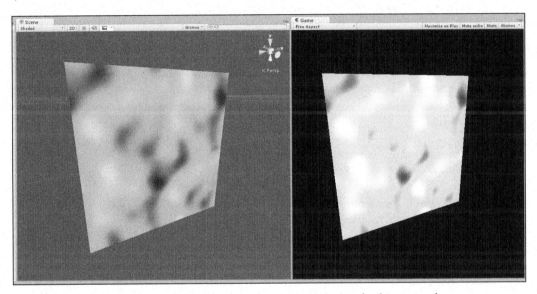

Animating texture mapping for a surface to create moving clouds, water, or lava

Code sample 1-6: material scroller:

```
//CLASS TO SCROLL TEXTURE ON PLANE. CAN BE USED FOR MOVING SKY
//------------------------------------------------
using UnityEngine;
using System.Collections;
//------------------------------------------------
[RequireComponent (typeof (MeshRenderer))] //Requires Renderer Filter
Component
public class MatScroller : MonoBehaviour
{
  //Public variables
  //------------------------------------------------
  //Reference to Horizontal Scroll Speed
```

```
public float HorizSpeed = 1.0f;

//Reference to Vertical Scroll Speed
public float VertSpeed = 1.0f;

//Reference to Min and Max Horiz and Vertical UVs to scroll between
public float HorizUVMin = 1.0f;
public float HorizUVMax = 2.0f;

public float VertUVMin = 1.0f;
public float VertUVMax = 2.0f;

//Private variables
//--------------------------------------------------
//Reference to Mesh Renderer Component
private MeshRenderer MeshR = null;

//Methods
//--------------------------------------------------
// Use this for initialization
void Awake ()
{
  //Get Mesh Renderer Component
  MeshR = GetComponent<MeshRenderer>();
}
//--------------------------------------------------
// Update is called once per frame
void Update ()
{
  //Scrolls texture between min and max
  Vector2 Offset = new Vector2((MeshR.material.mainTextureOffset.x >
HorizUVMax) ? HorizUVMin : MeshR.material.mainTextureOffset.x + Time.
deltaTime * HorizSpeed,
                  (MeshR.material.mainTextureOffset.y > VertUVMax)
? VertUVMin : MeshR.material.mainTextureOffset.y + Time.deltaTime *
VertSpeed);

  //Update UV coordinates
  MeshR.material.mainTextureOffset = Offset;
}
```

```
    //----------------------------------------------
}
    //----------------------------------------------
```

This code can be attached to a mesh object to animate its material. Simply set the HorizSpeed and VertSpeed variables from the object inspector to control the horizontal and vertical scroll speeds of the material.

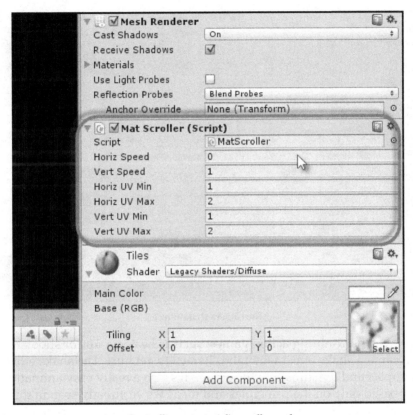

Controlling a material's scroll speed

The Unity project for this assignment can be found in this book's companion files in the `Chapter01/texture_animator` folder.

Camera shaking – animation effects

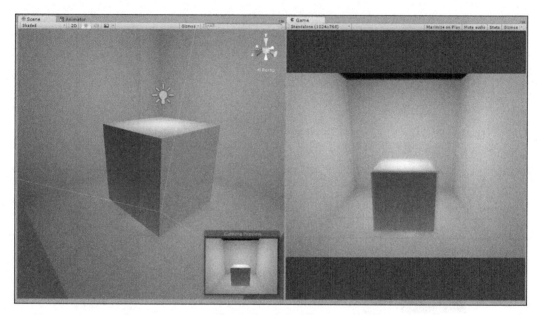

The camera shake effect

If you've played hard-hitting action games, such as beat 'em ups or shooters, you'll often see a camera shake effect when the characters get hurt. The shake effect adds a dramatic impact and dynamism to the action. It's also a really easy animation effect to achieve, based only on the principles and ideas we've already seen in this chapter. Consider code sample 1-7, which may be added to any scene camera to create a shake effect:

Code sample 1-7: camera shake:

```
using UnityEngine;
using System.Collections;
//---------------------
public class CameraShake : MonoBehaviour
{
  private Transform ThisTransform = null;

  //Total time for shaking in seconds
```

```csharp
public float ShakeTime = 2.0f;

//Shake amount - distance to offset in any direction
public float ShakeAmount = 3.0f;

//Speed of camera moving to shake points
public float ShakeSpeed = 2.0f;

//--------------------
// Use this for initialization
void Start ()
{
  //Get transform component
  ThisTransform = GetComponent<Transform>();

  //Start shaking
  StartCoroutine(Shake());
}
//--------------------
//Shake camera
public IEnumerator Shake()
{
  //Store original camera position
  Vector3 OrigPosition = ThisTransform.localPosition;

  //Count elapsed time (in seconds)
  float ElapsedTime = 0.0f;

  //Repeat for total shake time
  while(ElapsedTime < ShakeTime)
  {
    //Pick random point on unit sphere
    Vector3 RandomPoint = OrigPosition + Random.insideUnitSphere *
ShakeAmount;

    //Update Position
    ThisTransform.localPosition = Vector3.Lerp(ThisTransform.
localPosition, RandomPoint, Time.deltaTime * ShakeSpeed);

    //Break for next frame
    yield return null;

    //Update time
```

```
        ElapsedTime += Time.deltaTime;
    }

    //Restore camera position
    ThisTransform.localPosition = OrigPosition;
    }
    //---------------------
    }
    //---------------------
```

This code sample uses coroutines to fluctuate the position of the camera randomly over time within an imaginary spherical volume using the `Random.insideUnitSphere` variable. To use this code, just drag and drop the script onto a camera, and go!

> The Unity project for this assignment can be found in this book's companion files in the `Chapter01/camera_shake` folder.

Summary

This chapter considered animation abstractly, as a form of art, and as a science. We covered the types of animation that are most common in Unity games. In addition, we examined some core tasks and ideas in programmatic animation, including the ability to animate and change objects dynamically through code without relying on pre-scripted or predefined animations, which will engross you in much of this book. Although this chapter marks the end of our coverage of programmatic animation (at least in a dedicated way), coding and scripts will nevertheless find an important niche and presence throughout most of the upcoming chapters. The next chapter continues our journey, with us entering the world of 2D animation for sprites.

2

Sprite Animation

In this chapter, we enter the world of 2D game animation in Unity—specifically, sprite animation and its associated feature set, which is extensive. If you're planning on making 2D games, such as side-scrolling platformers or casual puzzle games for mobiles, or if you're creating animated GUIs and menu systems, then 2D animation will probably be highly important for your project.

A 2D side-scrolling platform game in action

Before getting started, however, let me elaborate further on the meaning of **2D**, as opposed to 3D animation, to clarify the scope of this chapter and the kind of animation we are concerned with here.

By 2D (short for two-dimensional), I mean only a specific kind of presentation, that is, any scene presented using either an orthographic camera or a camera showing objects in a planar or flat way, not allowing the user to rotate their view and observe events from other angles. In this sense, even a 3D scene may be part of a 2D game because 2D relates only to a scene's mode of display through cameras and not to any intrinsic properties of the scene. Even so, most of our 2D work will be related to sprite objects, a special 2D game object type supported by Unity. So, let's get started. Our aim in this chapter will be to create an animated sprite character that runs through the level, playing a run animation as he moves.

Sprites – importing and configuration

A **sprite** is a dedicated 2D object type in Unity. It lets you import a flat, regular texture for displaying a scene as if it were a cardboard prop or billboard. Sprites are useful for animated characters and props, such as the playable character in a side-scrolling platformer. 2D sprite animation works much like traditional **flip-book** animation, where key frame sketches are drawn on the pages of a book, one frame per page, and are played back to create animation by quickly turning the pages and observing the effect. There are two methods of importing and configuring animated sprites for your game, and this section covers both of them. The sprite objects used here are included in this book's companion files in the `Chapter02/assets` folder. So, open the assets and follow along with me. Let's start by considering two methods of importing sprites: importing individual sprites and importing a sprite atlas.

 More information about sprite objects can be found in the online Unity documentation at `http://docs.unity3d.com/ScriptReference/Sprite.html`.

Individual sprites

If you've created an animated sprite using separate image files for each frame of animation, you can simply drag and drop all the frames at once into the Unity Project panel for importing.

Importing animated sprites as separate files frame by frame

When you do this, each file is imported as a regular texture.

Imported running animation for a player character in the Unity Project panel

To convert them into sprites, select all the imported textures in the Project panel. From the Object Inspector, choose the **Sprite** option for the **Texture Type** setting. Make sure that **Sprite Mode** is set to **Single**, as each separate image represents a unique frame for the *same* sprite overall (that is, the same character). In addition, the **Generate Mip Maps** setting should be disabled so as to improve texture quality. Finally, the **Pivot** option for the sprite should be set to **Bottom**, the location of the feet of most character sprites. This is because the feet are where the character meets the ground plane and is effectively positioned within the scene. Afterwards, click on **Apply** to confirm.

Remember that you don't have to apply sprite settings to each texture individually. That would be tedious! Instead, you can select multiple textures in the Project panel and apply settings to all of them as a batch.

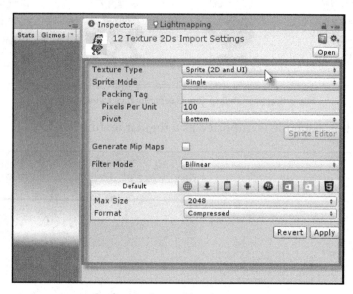

Configuring imported sprite textures

And that's it! The imported frames are now configured and ready for sprite animation in the scene. We'll see how to do that specifically later in this chapter. Next, let's see how to import a slightly different kind of sprite.

The sprite atlas

Sometimes, your sprites may already be compiled together into a single sprite sheet, called a **texture atlas**. In other words, all the frames in an animation may be bundled together into regular rows and columns inside a single texture file, as opposed to many separate files. These kinds of sprite sheets are also supported by Unity, but they require some additional setup and tweaking at the import stage.

A sprite atlas texture

To import the sprite atlas, simply drag and drop the texture into the Unity Project panel. It'll be imported as a regular texture file. This will be shown inside the Project panel.

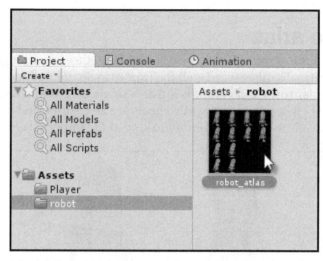

By default, sprite atlas textures are imported as regular textures

After the import, you'll need to configure the texture properly to work as a sprite. To do this, select the texture in the Project panel. From the Object Inspector, choose **Sprite** for the **Texture Type** option. Then choose **Multiple** for the **Sprite Mode** option. This is because the texture file contains multiple frames, not just one. Disable the **Generate Mip Maps** checkbox for optimal texture quality and then click on **Apply**.

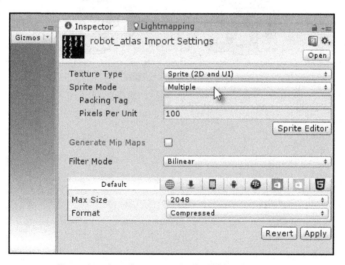

Preparing the atlas texture in the Object Inspector

Choosing **Multiple** for the **Sprite Mode** option signals that multiple frames exist within the texture, but Unity still doesn't know precisely where they are in the texture. To define this, the **Sprite Editor** can be used. This tool is accessed by clicking on the **Sprite Editor** button from the Object Inspector when the texture is selected in the Project panel. From the **Sprite Editor** dialog, you can manually draw the boundaries for each sprite by simply clicking and dragging a box around each one in the image. Alternatively, you can automatically generate sprite slices from a tiling pattern. For the robot texture provided with this book's companion files, each sprite is in a 512 x 512 pixel grid. To generate slices for this, click on the **Slice** button in the top-left corner of the **Sprite Editor** window.

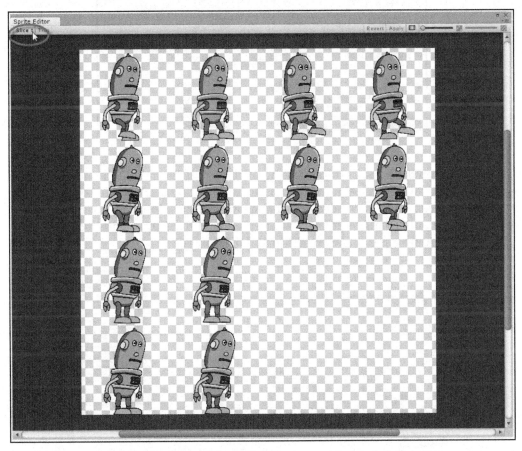

Click on the slice button in the Sprite Editor to generate slices from the atlas

After clicking on the **Slice** button, a configuration popup appears. Fill in the slice parameters to generate slices for the frames in the atlas. For the robot texture provided here, the **Slice** type should be set to **Grid** (instead of **Automatic**), since the sprites are arranged in a grid inside the image. **Pixel Size** should be **512 x 512**, and **Pivot** should be set to **Bottom** to position the pivot at the character's feet.

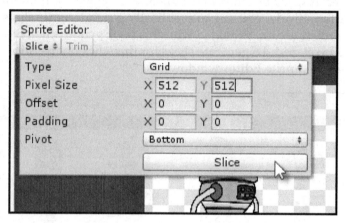

Generating slices from a grid

After clicking on the **Slice** button from the **Slice** popup, Unity will divide the texture atlas into separate sprites, each of which is surrounded by a selectable border. If required, you can select each slice and change its settings. However, for the robot texture, the default arrangement can be accepted, and the **Apply** button can be clicked on from the top toolbar in the **Sprite Editor** window.

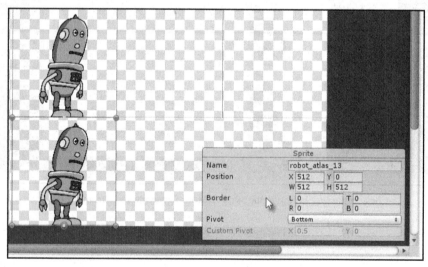

The slices are now created

Clicking on **Apply** from the **Sprite Editor** window generates a sequence of sprite objects, which appear in the Project panel as independent entities and are now ready for animation.

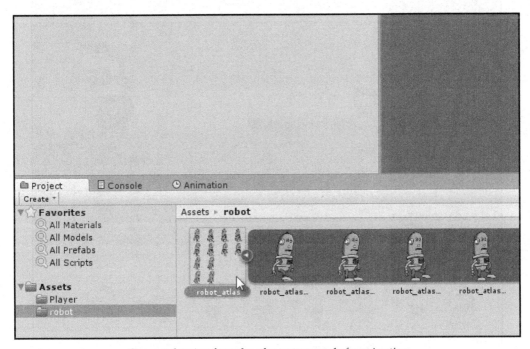

Generated sprites from the atlas texture, ready for animation

Animation with sprites

After you've imported a set of sprite objects, either as individual images or as atlas textures, you're ready to start animating with them using a single technique. Achieving this is really simple, at least initially. From the Unity Project panel, just select all sprites that go together as a complete animation sequence, and then drag and drop them as one into the Scene Hierarchy panel. Dropping them into the scene or game tabs won't work; it must be inside the hierarchy panel. For example, drag and drop the player run animation sequence (from this book's files) into the scene. When you do this, Unity displays a **Save** dialog, prompting you to create a new animation sequence asset (.anim is the file extension).

Assign the animation a name (such as `PlayerRun.anim`) and then click on **Save**.

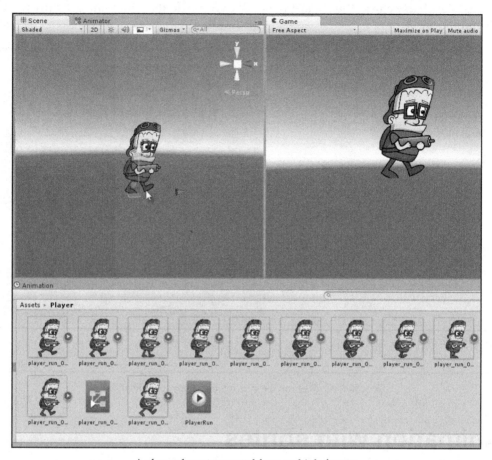

A player character created from multiple frames

A sprite object is created in the scene, and it should be visible in the **Scene** and **Game** tabs. If it's not, make sure that the object is positioned within the view of the camera. And that's all there is to creating an initial animation sequence. If you test your scene, your sprite character will now be animated, running through all the images in the sequence. This is achieved because Unity has performed a series of configuration steps behind the scenes. Specifically, Unity created a new `Animation Clip` (`.anim`) asset that defines the key frame sequence. Secondly, Unity has created a Mecanim controller to initiate an animation playback as the level begins, and to control the playback speed. Thirdly, Unity has added an animator component to the sprite object in the scene to link the object to its animation data. By default, however, the animation created may not appear exactly as you want. So, in the subsequent sections, we'll see how we can tweak the animation.

Sprite animation is too slow or too fast

If your sprite animation is playing too fast or too slow, then you'll need to edit the sprite Mecanim graph (Mecanim is covered in depth in later chapters). The animation speed for sprites can be changed quickly and easily. To achieve this, select the sprite object in the scene. From the Object Inspector, double-click on the **Animation Controller** asset inside the **Controller** slot of the **Animator** component.

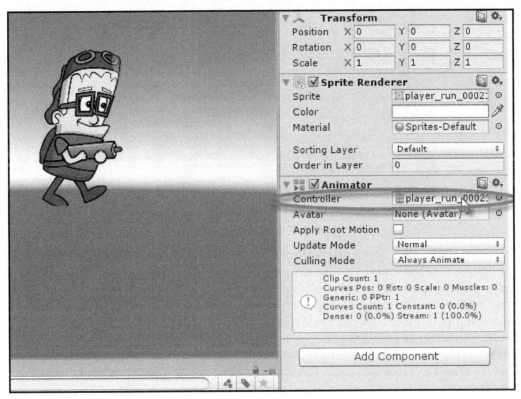

Accessing the sprite Animation Controller

Double-clicking on the sprite **Animation Controller** will open the Mecanim graph for the sprite. Here, the animation speed can be controlled. This graph contains several nodes connected together.

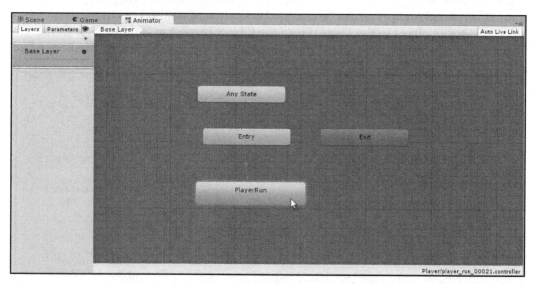

The Mecanim graph for the animated sprite

From the graph, click on the **PlayerRun** (default) node, which represents the sprite animation, to select it and view its properties in the Object Inspector. For the player sprite graphic (included in this book's companion files), this node represents a full walk animation. The animation speed is controlled using the **Speed** setting. In it, **0** means stopped, **1** means the default speed, **0.5** means half speed, **2** means double speed, and so on. If your animation is too slow, then increase the **Speed** value, and if it is too fast, then reduce the **Speed** value. For my player character animation, I set the speed to **2** double speed. Once you're done, just replay your game to see the effect.

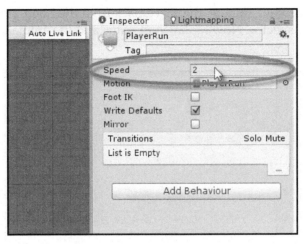

Changing the animation speed

Animation shouldn't be looping

By default, sprite animations play on a loop cycle; that is, they play again and again without an end. When the animation playback completes a cycle, it simply returns to the beginning and plays again. This may be exactly what you need in some cases, but not always. Sometimes, you may want the animation to play only once and then stop. If so, you'll need to access the animation data (inside the .anim asset) and adjust its properties. To do this, select the sprite animation asset in the Project panel. Animation assets feature a **Play** icon and match the name you gave the animation during its creation.

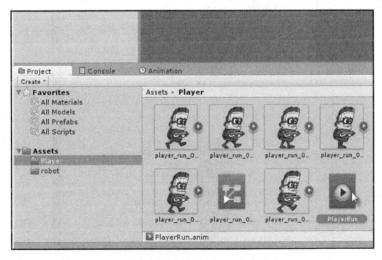

Selecting an animation asset

After the asset is selected, remove the checkmark from the **Loop Time** checkbox inside the Object Inspector. Now replay your game and the animation will play only once.

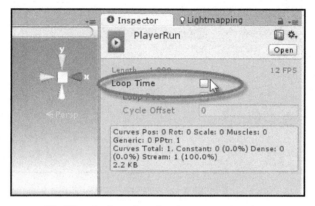

Disabling the loop time for play-once animations

Frames play in the wrong order

If your sprite animation features many frames, it's possible that Unity arranged them in the wrong order while generating the animation, resulting in some frames appearing before or after they should. If this happens, you'll need to edit the animation data itself, through the **Animation** window. This window can be accessed by going to **Window | Animation** from the application menu.

Accessing the Animation window

With the **Animation** window visible in the editor, select the sprite object in the scene, and its animation data will show up automatically in the timeline. The timeline represents the total duration of the animation, from start to end. The diamond-shaped symbols dotted evenly along the timeline represent key frames, in which the sprite image changes. You can select a specific key frame in the timeline by clicking on it. Then, you can also view its properties for the sprite in the Object Inspector. For example, with the player character animation, at time equal to **0:06**, the **player_run_00013** sprite is shown. The **Sprite** field in the Object Inspector is highlighted in red to show that the field is animated and changes over time.

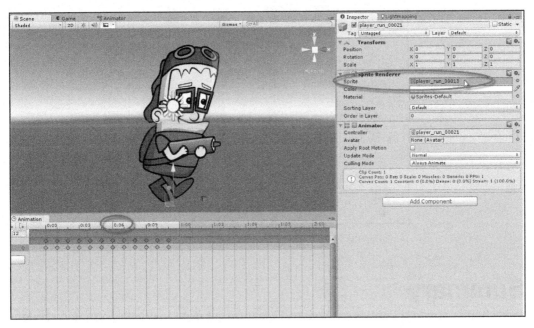

Viewing key frames for sprite animation

When you select a key frame from the timeline in which the wrong image is shown for the sprite at that time, you can easily correct it by just clicking on the **Sprite** field in the Object Inspector and picking a new sprite object from the sprite browser. Unity will automatically record, or understand, that the newly selected sprite should be displayed for that key frame instead.

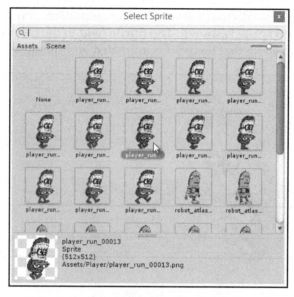

Using the sprite browser to correct animation frames

Summary

This chapter covered Unity's extensive 2D feature set used to create animated sprites. Sprites can be imported on a frame-by-frame basis from separate files, or as a texture atlas containing many frames together. In either case, frames can easily be assembled into an animated sequence, and Unity's animation tools (such as Mecanim and the **Animation** window) can be used to repair the most common issues, such as those concerning animation speed, looping, and misplaced frames.

Using the assets provided with this chapter (including the player character asset), you should now be able to quickly and effectively create an animated character playing a run animation. In addition, you can use the object Mover script created in the previous chapter to move the animated sprite object along an axis in the scene, while also playing its run animation to simulate a complete run cycle. A completed project that does this is available in the companion files in the Chapter02\ AnimatedChar folder. In the next chapter, the Unity **Animation** window, as well as other tools, will be explored in more detail.

3
Native Animation

Unity is not regarded as a content creation tool, but rather a compositional tool. That is, it is typically known as a **game engine** in which premade assets (assets made in other applications) are imported and configured to produce a final game. However, despite this largely correct understanding, Unity does offer a range of asset creation tools, especially concerning animation. These are called native animation features. They include the following:

- The **Unity animation editor** for rigid body animation, such as doors that open, camera fly-throughs, elevator platforms, and more
- The **Shuriken particle system**, for rain, snow, fireworks, sparkles, and other cases of intangible animation with many moving parts
- Both of these are considered thoroughly in this chapter.

The Animation window – creating a fly-through

The **Animation** window is a fully featured animation editor used to create pre-scripted key frame animation on any numerical properties of GameObjects, such as position, rotation, and scale. In short, it lets you animate GameObjects over time, saving the final animation data as a separate and self-contained asset in the Project panel, called an **animation clip**. If you want to create doors that open and close by rotating on their hinges, elevator platforms that move up and down, rotating floors, moving cars, or enemy spaceships flying around, among other things, then the **Animation** window may be exactly what you need.

To demonstrate its functionality, in this section, we will create a camera fly-through around an environment. However, it's important to recognize that in creating a fly-through, as we will, a more general and abstract toolset is demonstrated—a toolset that can be reused and applied to create animations for practically any purpose, not just camera fly-throughs. To get started then, you may use your own environment, if you have one, or else open the starting project for this section, which is included in this book's companion files inside the `Chapter03/FlyThroughStart` folder. Once you have an environment and a camera, you're ready to follow along.

Creating an environment for a camera fly-through

 The complete project for this section can be found in the companion files inside the `Chapter03/FlyThroughEnd` folder.

To access the **Animation** window to create key frame animation, go to **Window |
Animation** from the main menu (or press *Ctrl + 6* on the keyboard). Be sure to
select **Animation** and *not* **Animator**.

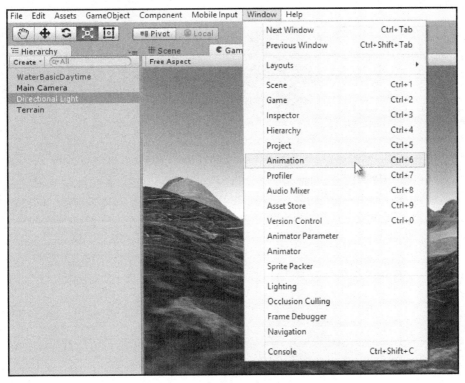

Accessing the Animation window from the main menu

The **Animation** window is best viewed in horizontal alignment, so I typically dock the window at the bottom of the interface, underneath the **Game** and **Scene** tabs. To do this, just drag and drop the **Animation** window into the Project panel or Console area, over the tab titles.

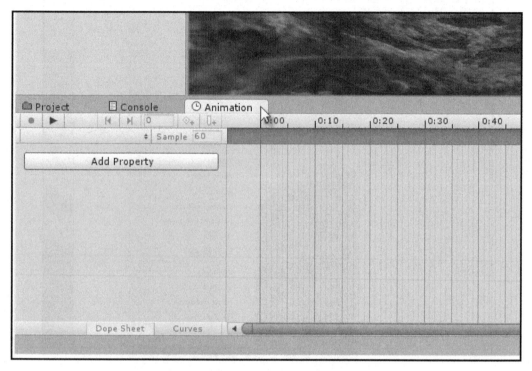

Docking the Animation window at the bottom of the interface

To create a key frame animation for a GameObject, select the object to animate in the scene, or by name through the Hierarchy panel. Then click on the **Add Property** button from the **Animation** window. For an animated camera fly-through, select the scene camera and then choose **Add Property** from the **Animation** window. After you've clicked on this button, Unity prompts you with a **Save** dialog for a physical location within the project folder where the animation data (**Animation Clip**) should be named and saved. Name the animation `CameraFlyAnim.anim`, and select the **Assets** folder to save inside the root of the project.

Creating a new animation clip asset

On creating a new animation clip, Unity actually performs multiple processes behind the scenes. First, it creates two assets: an **Animation Clip** asset (containing all of the key frame data) and an **Animation Controller** asset, which links to the Mecanim system. Further, an **Animator** component is added to the **Camera** object in the scene, which refers to the **Animation Controller** asset, which in turn is responsible for playing the animation clip data automatically when the scene begins. More details on Mecanim will be covered in the next chapter. For now, it's sufficient to consider only the **Animation Controller** as the active force that will initiate the animation playback.

Creating a new animation clip, with an autogenerated Animation Controller

Next, having created an **Animation Clip** asset, we'll need to define an animation. Unity can record key frame data for any numerical property. In other words, any field on an object represented by numbers, such as position and rotation, can be animated and blended over time. To animate a camera fly-through, we'll need to record both the position and rotation of the camera as they change over time. To do this, click on the **Add Property** button inside the **Animation** window, and from the context menu that appears, choose the channels to animate. Specifically, click on the + button and go to **Transform**. Then you can go to either the **Position** channel or the **Rotation** channel. This adds two channels to the **Animation** window (position and rotation), which can now be animated. A channel is simply any property for which we can add key frames.

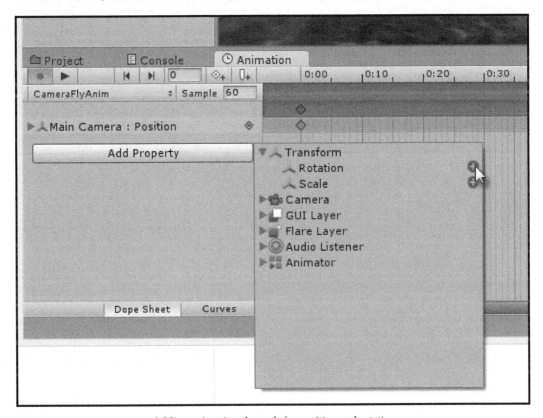

Adding animation channels for position and rotation

By default, two key frames are autogenerated for both the position and rotation channels—one frame at animation start (time: 0 seconds) and one at the end (time: 1 second). Key frames are represented graphically by grey diamonds inside the timeline view. You can also click and drag the mouse inside the time-measure bar (at the top of the timeline) to position the play head of the animation, previewing the animation at any time. By default, however, both the start and end key frames for the camera are identical, which means that it will not change during the animation.

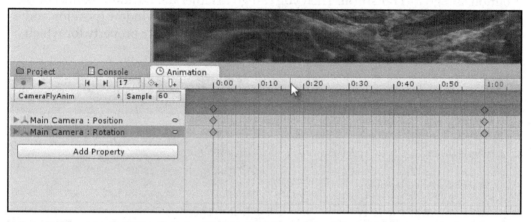

Setting the animation play head to preview animation frames

You can create a key frame manually to record the state of any channel (or all channels) for the camera at any time in the animation. This can be done by first clicking on the channel to record, using the left-hand column in the **Animation** window (**Channel List**). Then move the time slider (click and drag) to the relevant time, and finally click on the **Add Key Frame** button from the **Animation** window toolbar. This inserts a new key frame into the timeline at the location of the play head. Remember that multiple key frames can be added for multiple channels simultaneously by pressing *Shift* and selecting the channels in the channel list; that is, hold down the *Shift* key on the keyboard while clicking on the channels. You can also click and drag the key frame diamond icons into the timeline to reposition them for different times, as well as duplicate them with *Ctrl* + *C* and *Ctrl* + *V*. You can also delete selected key frames with the *Backspace* or *Delete* key.

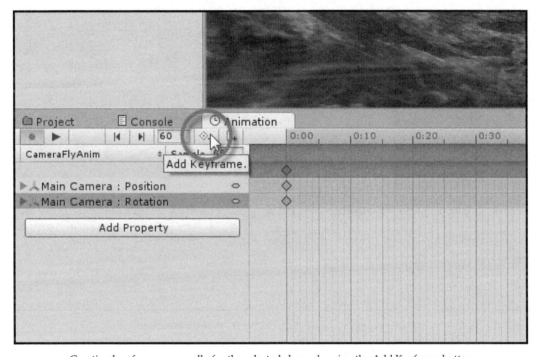

Creating key frames manually for the selected channels using the Add Keyframe button

Creating key frames manually, as we've seen, is a legitimate method of defining animation, but it's easier to have Unity generate key frames automatically for us, based on movements of, and changes in, objects in the scene. Creating a camera fly-through using this method is easy; position the animation play head to frame **0** in the **Animation** window, and then simply move and rotate the camera object in the scene to its starting position and orientation. Unity will automatically record the position and rotation channels for the camera at that time. Then click and drag the play head further to time **0:15** in the **Animation** window, and move and rotate the camera in the scene again to a new position and rotation for that time. Unity will generate a new set of key frames in response to the selected time. Repeat this process of key frame generation, defining position and rotation values for the camera at times 0:30, 0:45, and 1:00 to generate a key for each time.

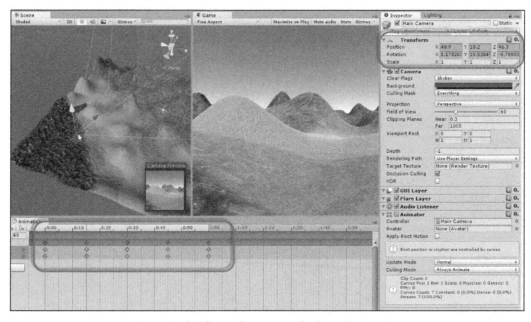

Generating key frames for a camera fly-through animation

Try to make the first and last key frames identical (using *Ctrl + C* and *Ctrl + V*), copying and pasting the first key frame to the end time, at time **1:00**. This means that the animation will end with the same appearance as it begins, making it loopable, that is, the kind of animation that plays seamlessly again and again in a loop. When the animation is fully defined to your satisfaction, try it out. Click on **Play** in the Unity toolbar, and the animation will play automatically, due to the **Animator** component. If the animation plays too fast or too slow, or if it doesn't loop, refer to the previous chapter (*Chapter 2, Sprite Animation*) to control sprite animation speed and looping.

Congratulations! You've just created a camera fly-through animation.

Animating multiple objects together

The camera fly-through animation created in the previous section involves animating only one object, namely the camera. But there'll be times when you'll need to animate multiple objects in sync, such as the wheels of a car rotating independently as the car moves forward. In this case, the car moves forward, but the wheels should also turn as they move with the rest of the car. To achieve this kind of multipart animation, you should first bring all relevant objects together under a single parent object. For the car example, all the wheels, the chassis, and engine will belong to a single parent, named **Car**.

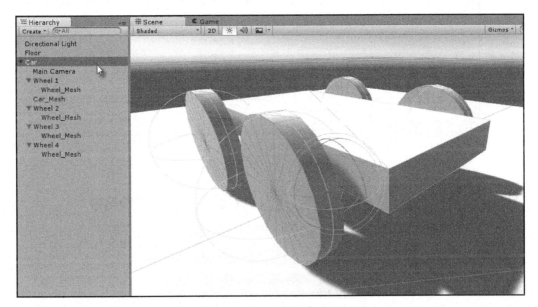

Preparing a multipart object for animation

The sample car project is included in this book's companion files in the Chapter03/CarAnim folder.

When an animation clip is added to a parent object instead of a child object, you can animate channels on any (or all) of its children too, giving you control over multiple objects as far as the animation is concerned. In the animation editor window, click on **Add Property** and select the channels to add from the popup menu. The menu features channels across all children.

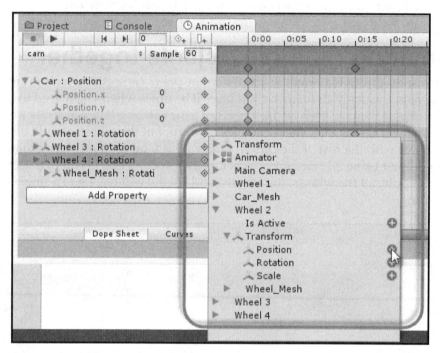

Adding transformation channels in child objects for animation

Invoking functions from animations

Frequently, you'll need to link animations with the script and game logic. Specifically, when animation playback reaches a specific frame or time, or when an animation begins or ends, you may want something else to happen in script, even on a completely different object. In the camera fly-through animation for example, we may want to show a message on the screen saying "**Welcome!**", when the fly-through animation ends. There are many ways to handle this type of requirement. One way is to run a function in script when a frame shows up in the animation. To create this kind of connectivity between animation and script, we'll need an animation event.

The complete Unity project for an animation event is included in this book's companion files in the `Chapter03/AnimationEvents` folder.

To get started with calling functions from animations, create a new C# script file or edit an existing file. Add a function of any name that returns void and either; has no arguments, or accepts a string, a float, an integer, or a GameObject. See the following code sample, which accepts no arguments and shows a GUI canvas object when called, to display a welcome message, which should happen when the camera fly-through animation completes. The script file should be attached to the camera object in the scene.

 More information on animation events can be found at the online Unity documentation at `docs.unity3d.com/Manual/animeditor-AnimationEvents.html`.

```csharp
//---------------------------------------------
using UnityEngine;
using System.Collections;
using UnityEngine.UI;
//---------------------------------------------
public class ShowMessage : MonoBehaviour
{
  //Reference to GUI canvas to show on event
  public Canvas UICanvas = null;

  //Function to be called from an Animation Event
  void ShowWelcomeMessage()
  {
    //Enable canvas to show message
    UICanvas.gameObject.SetActive(true);
  }
}
//---------------------------------------------
```

To create a link between the animation and the ShowWelcomeMessage function, open the **Animation** window and right-click on the grey bar above the final key frame at time 1:00 but below the time header. When you do this, a context menu appears, showing the option to create an animation event at the selected key frame, like this:

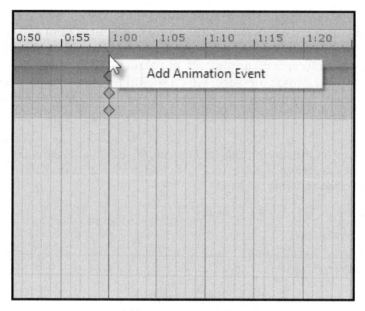

Adding an animation event

Click on **Add Animation Event** from the context menu. After this, the **Edit Animation Event** dialog appears, featuring a drop-down list control. This allows you to choose the function to call duration the event. If your custom function is not shown in the list as an option, make sure that all the relevant script files are attached to the animated game object.

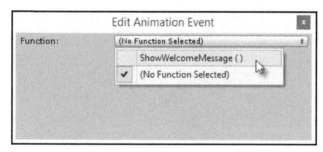

Selecting a function to call during an animation event

Close the **Edit Animation Event** dialog, and now a white marker will be added to the Animation timeline, indicating the time of the function call. The marker can be edited, deleted, and moved, just like a regular key frame object.

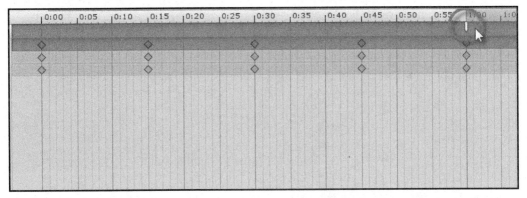

Invoking an animation event from an animation timeline

And that's it! The animation event will now run automatically on the animated object at runtime whenever the play head hits the final frame. Click on **Play** in the Unity toolbar to give the project a test run.

 Remember that the UI Canvas public member of the ShowMessage script should reference a valid UI Canvas object in the scene. See the companion files folder Chapter3\AnimationEvents. More information on UI Canvas can be found in the online Unity documentation at http://docs.unity3d.com/ScriptReference/Canvas.html.

Showing a Welcome! message when an animation ends

Particle Systems

Particle systems are primarily responsible for creating special effects and animation where many parts or things must move together as something cohesive, such as rain, snow, sparkles, fairy dust, flocks of birds, swarms of bees, and more. They're also used to simulate intangible things, such as light rays, dust, ghosts, holograms, and others.

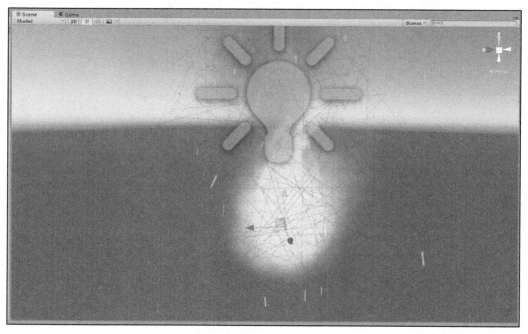

A fire particle system in action

Unity 5 ships with a wide range of premade particle systems that can simply be dragged and dropped into a scene to create the most common particle effects, such as explosions, fire, steam, and smoke. To access these effects, import the Particle Systems asset package into your project by going to **Assets | Import Package | ParticleSystems** from the application menu. After this import, all the premade systems will be available by going to **Assets | ParticleSystems | Prefabs** from the Unity Project panel.

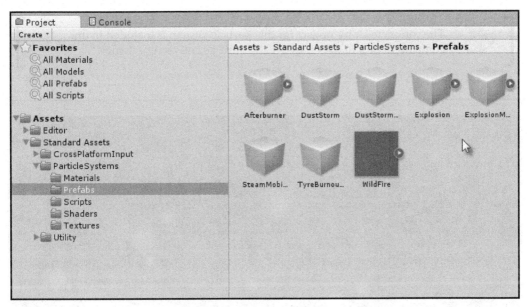

Unity 5 ships with many premade particle systems

Despite the differences between them, all particle systems have three features in common. The first is an **emitter** element, which is like a hose, or portal, from which particles are emitted or spewed. The second is the **particle** itself—the small things or pieces that the emitter generates. For rain systems, each rain drop is a particle; for snow, each snow flake; for a flock of birds, each bird is a particle; and so on. Finally, once a particle is emitted, it has a **lifetime** that defines the duration for which it exists, and also a trajectory or velocity that defines what happens to the particle during its lifetime (how it moves, how fast it travels, and so on). Therefore, creating a particle system for animation is all about defining how these three elements work together. Consider the next section for a practical project—creating a particle system from the ground up using the Shuriken System.

Starting a firefly particle system

A common particle system included in games, especially in fantasy RPGs, is fireflies. If you're navigating through a dark forest at night, or are wading through a treacherous swamp in the mist, you'll often find small, bright fireflies hovering around. They don't really do anything functional in terms of the gameplay; that is, they neither harm nor benefit you. Rather, their purpose is entirely cosmetic and emotional. They convey an atmosphere and setting. In this system, a group of bright fireflies moves around slowly and calmly, each fly following its own unique velocity.

The complete Unity project for this particle system is included in the companion files in the Chapter03/ParticleSystems folder.

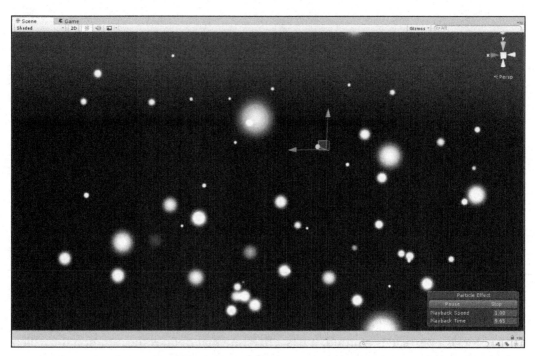

Creating a firefly particle system with shuriken

The standard Unity particle package doesn't include the firefly effect, so we'll create it here. To do this, we'll use the Unity Shuriken System. Let's create a new particle system by going to **GameObject | ParticleSystem** from the application menu. Choosing this creates a new default particle system object in the scene. When selected, the particle system will automatically play in the scene viewport.

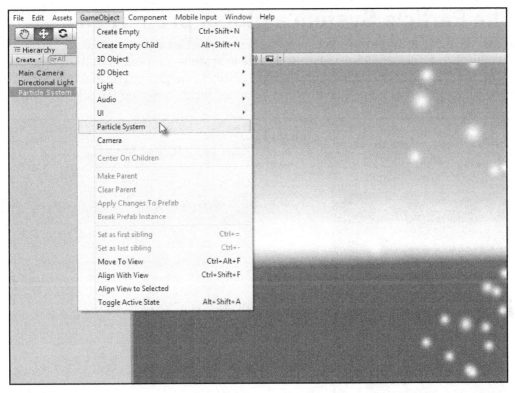

Creating a particle system with Shuriken

 For this project, I've set the scene lighting to night time, or just after sunset. To do this, simply create a new scene and rotate the default directional light to face upwards. The Unity 5 default skybox will automatically respond to the light orientation.

The Particle System's global properties

When the Particle System is selected in the scene, you can view its properties from the Shuriken Editor, which appears as a Particle System component in the Object Inspector. This editor is divided into several distinct categories. The main global properties control general attributes and behavior for the selected Particle System.

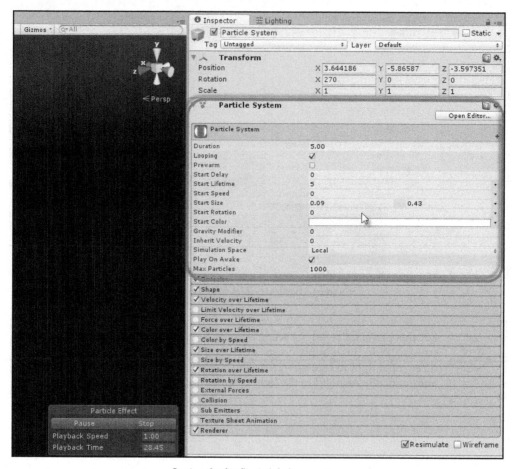

Setting the fireflies' global properties

The **Duration** value defines the total length of the particle system animation before it begins again and loops. For the firefly effect, the **Start Speed** value has been set to 0, because the speed and motion will vary on a per particle basis and will be overridden, or controlled, by more advanced settings in the Shuriken Editor. **Start Size** controls the overall size of a generated particle. This field has been changed from a single constant value (making all particles the same size) to a random value for each particle, chosen between a minimum value and a maximum value (allowing each particle to get a different size). This gives us size variation among the fireflies in the system. To access this setting, click on the right-hand-side arrow for the **Start Size** field and choose **Random Between Two Constants** from the context menu.

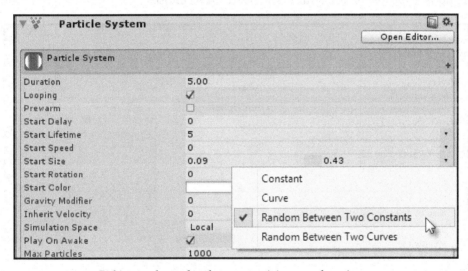

Picking random values between a minimum and maximum

Emitter shape and emission rate

As mentioned, every Particle System has an emitter, a spawn point at which new particles are generated. The emitter itself has a shape. It can be flat, a point, a cube, a sphere, or a custom mesh, and it represents the surface area or volume inside which the particles are generated. The exact point on the surface is randomly selected for each particle. To control the shape of the Emitter, expand the **Shape** tab in the Shuriken Editor, making sure that there's a checkmark in the **Shape** box. For the firefly system, all flies should be generated within a spherical volume. I set the radius of the sphere to 2.5 (meters). The **Radius** size is not essential, but a value that looks right and is appropriate for your scene needs to be chosen.

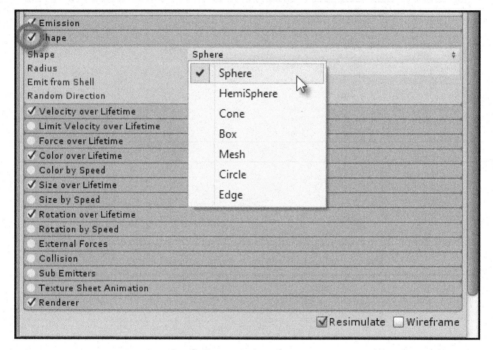

Setting an emitter shape

Next, let's expand the Emission section in the Shuriken Editor. This controls the frequency, or the rate at which new particles are generated from the Emitter per second. When generating fireflies, it's important not to cause too dense or thick a generation of particles. I set **Emission Rate** to **18.5**.

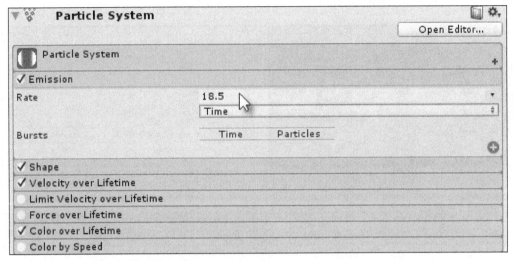

Setting the emission rate

Particle Renderer

Every particle in the system shares the same renderer, or appearance. The appearance settings for particles are controlled by the **Renderer** section of the Shuriken editor. The **Render Mode** field controls how the particle is displayed, and it mainly consists of two types: **Billboard** and **Mesh**. Billboard particles are made from a quad mesh with a texture assigned. Mesh particles are composed from more complex meshes other than quads, and you can use any mesh imported into the project. In addition to the **Render Mode** setting, a particle needs a material to be assigned to the particle mesh.

For particles you can use any material, but the firefly system will use a premade material provided as part of the default Unity Particle assets (which can be imported by going to **Assets | Import Package | ParticleSystems** from the application menu). The material I chose was **ParticleAfterburner**. You can simply drag and drop this material into the **Material** slot in the Object Inspector.

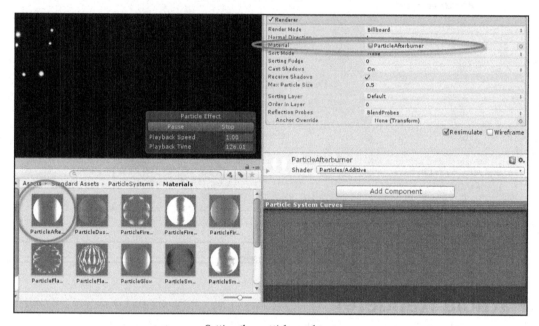

Setting the particle renderer

Particle velocity

One of the most critical features of the behavior of the firefly particle system is that each particle should move on its own trajectory. This is the case because each particle is supposed to be a separate and independent firefly, which is only part of a larger system of flies because of its proximity to other flies. The velocity of a particle during its lifetime is controlled by the **Velocity over Lifetime** section. When this section is expanded in the Object Inspector, you will be presented with three constant values for the x, y, and z axes. Together, these define a three-component vector, indicating the direction and speed at which all particles should travel. Therefore, three constant values are inappropriate for the firefly system because they cause *all* flies to travel in the same direction.

To randomize the direction of each fly, we'll need to change the Velocity mode from **Constant** to **Random Between Two Curves**. To change this, click on the downward-pointing arrow in the top-right corner of the **Velocity over Lifetime** section. If the options are ghosted or faded, ensure that the **Velocity over Lifetime** checkbox is enabled.

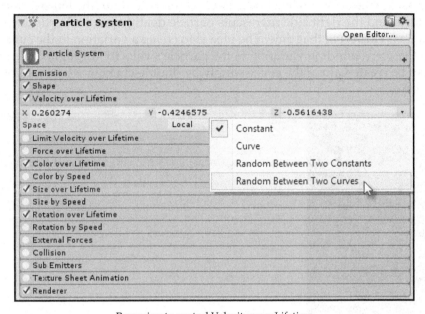

Preparing to control Velocity over Lifetime

By using two curves, a complete range of minimum and maximum velocity values can be set for each particle as it travels throughout its lifetime. To set the curves, click on an axis in the inspector to toggle its visibility as a graph in the Preview panel of the Object Inspector. View each axis one at a time by clicking on it. From the Preview panel, double-click to plot points on the line, and then click on the plot points and drag to reshape the curves. The Horizontal axis refers to time (the left side represents particle birth and the right side represents particle death), and the Vertical axis refers to the value (velocity) at that time. The idea is to create a variation in the curve to produce the corresponding variation in the particle's velocity throughout its lifetime. Points can be created along the curve simply by double-clicking wherever you want to add them.

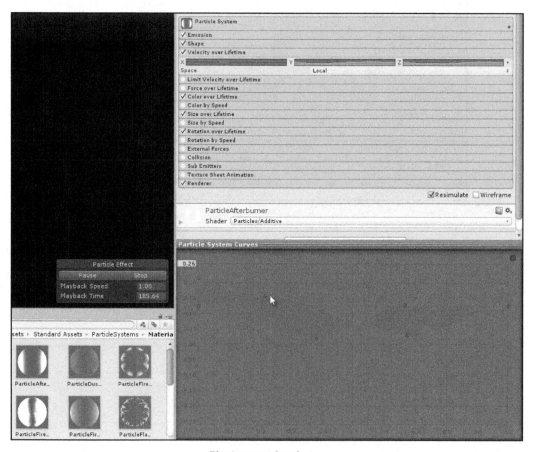

Plotting particle velocity

After creating the first curve, repeat the procedure for the remaining axes.
Once completed, the particles will move independently.

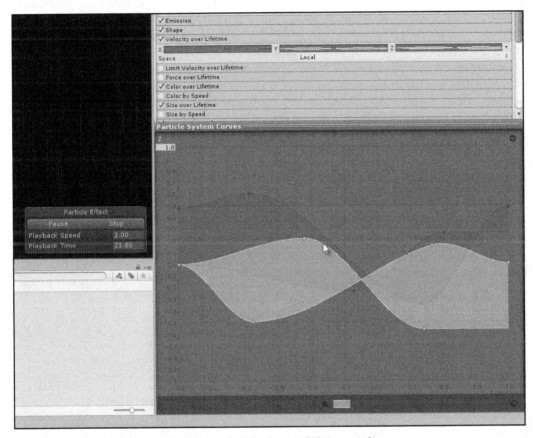

Completing the Velocity over Lifetime graph

Particle color and disappearance

To complete the firefly system, we should change the way the particles are born and die within the system. By default, particles are born by popping into existence, and then also die by simply popping out of existence. This produces a hard and binary transition between something existing and not existing, resulting in an unbelievable appearance for the system as a whole. This is because particles are visible in one moment and vanish in the next. To solve this, we can use the **Color over Lifetime** section, changing how the color of a particle fluctuates over its lifetime. This is important because a significant part of a particle color includes its alpha channel, or alpha transparency. Consequently, by controlling color, we can fade in and fade out particles with alpha.

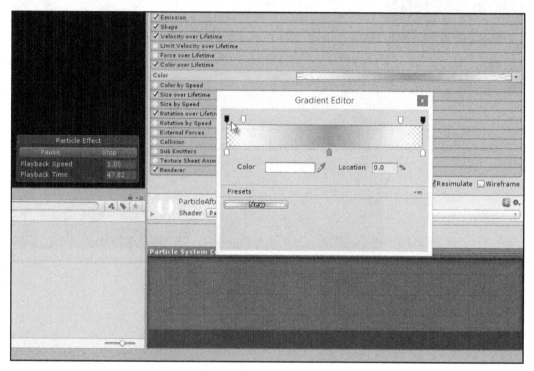

Controlling particle transparency with Color over Lifetime

To control the color throughout a particle's lifetime, click on the color gradient swatch inside the **Color over Lifetime** section, in the Object Inspector. This displays the **Gradient Editor** dialog. From here, you can view the color of a particle across its lifetime through a gradient control. The control spans the horizontal axis; the left side represents particle birth, and the right side represents particle death. The underside of the gradient bar charts the hue (color) of the particle, and the top side of the gradient bar charts transparency. You can control transparency by clicking at the top of the gradient to insert a bookmark slider at the mouse's position, and then clicking on the slider itself to set its alpha for that time (0 means transparent and 255 means fully visible). Insert two bookmarks at the beginning and end of the gradient to set the particle transparency to 0, marking the particle's birth and death respectively. Then insert two further bookmarks between 0 and 1 to raise the particle visibility to 255 to make particles fully visible. This results in particles that fade in at birth and fade out at death. This produces a smoother and tidier transition between particles as they enter and leave the system.

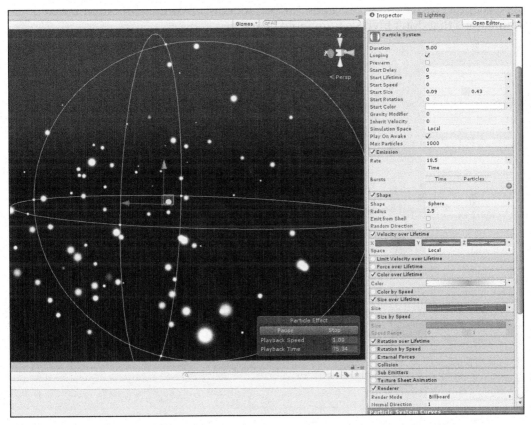

The final firefly system

Congratulations! You've just completed the firefly particle system, which can be used in a variety of games and circumstances. Now is a great time to create a prefab of the system, making it easier to drag and drop it into any of your scenes.

Summary

This chapter covered both the native Unity **Animation** window for developing in-game animations within Unity, and particle systems for creating animations with many moving parts. The Animation Editor produces the **Animation Clip** data, which defines a set of key frames plotting change over time, and these are compatible (as we'll see later) with the Mecanim System. Particle Systems, by contrast, are entirely procedural and do not save their animation data to key frames. Rather, animation is created dynamically within those systems at runtime, based on graph-based input specified using the Shuriken Editor in the Object Inspector. This allows particle systems to display an impressive degree of flexibility. In the next chapter, we'll explore Mecanim further, looking at various Mecanim-based animations that don't involve humanoid characters.

4
Noncharacter Animation with Mecanim

This chapter enters the world of Mecanim animation by explaining in depth how to create an interactive scene, complete with movable objects. Specifically, we'll create a scene where the player (in first-person mode) can press a button or lever to open a door elsewhere. This simple scenario will feature interactivity (the player presses a button), and in response, a door animation will play (a door rotates on its hinges in response to the button press). By creating this project, we'll explore the Mecanim animation system in Unity and see how to create interactivity without any traditional scripting. Let's jump in and get started.

Preparing a scene with the prototyping assets

The animation activity covered in this chapter will begin from a premade scene and project, which is included in this book's companion files in the `Chapter04/DoorAnim` folder. The scene contains some props and assets to work with, and it was assembled quickly using the Unity 5 prototyping assets, which feature many prefabs and objects (such as floors and stairs) for easy building of sample scenes.

I will take that sample scene as the starting point, as shown in the following screenshot. However, you can build your own level to achieve the same purpose and follow along with this chapter, if you prefer. To import the sample assets package, just go to **Assets | Import Package | Prototyping** from the application menu.

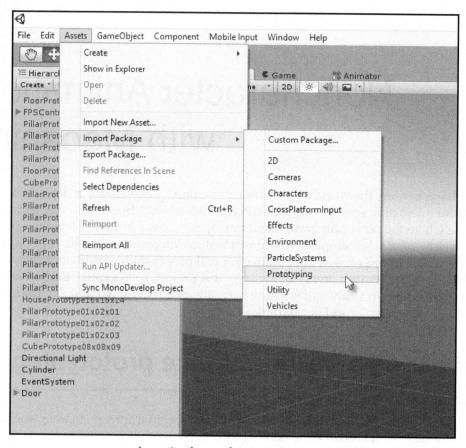

Importing the sample prototyping assets

Once the prototyping assets are imported, you can drag and drop the premade prefabs into the scene and start building an environment. The prototyping prefabs are included in **Standard Assets | Prototyping | Prefabs**.

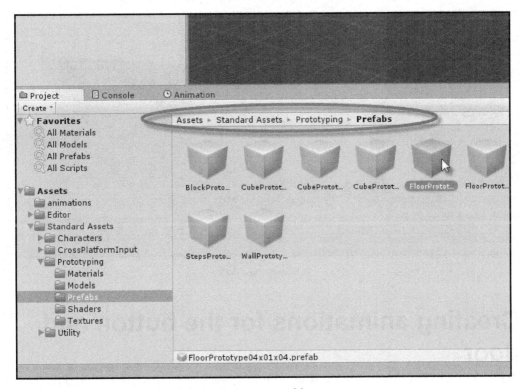

Prototyping prefabs

Here is the scene we'll be using for the animation project. It includes a button that can be pushed to unlock and open a door, leading to a different part of the environment.

A button and a door

Creating animations for the button and door

Before we start working with Mecanim directly, we'll need raw animation data from which to work; that is, we'll need two complete animations, one for the button, and one for the door. When the button is pushed, the door will open. Therefore, we'll need one animation for the button as it moves inward in its socket when pushed, and then returns to its neutral position. We'll also need a door-open animation so that the door rotates around its hinge, opening outwards. The latter should play only after the button is pushed. Both of these animations may be created directly inside the Unity editor using the **Animation** window, as explained in the previous chapter. For this reason, I'll cover the animation process here only in brief.

To create the button-push animation, select the button object in the scene, either in the viewport or in the hierarchy, and then switch to the **Animation** window. This can be accessed by going to **Window | Animation** from the main menu, or by pressing *Ctrl + 6* on the keyboard. From the **Animation** window, insert key frames for the `Transform.Position` track along the timeline: at the beginning, in the middle, and at the end, time 0 seconds, 0.5 seconds, and 1 second.

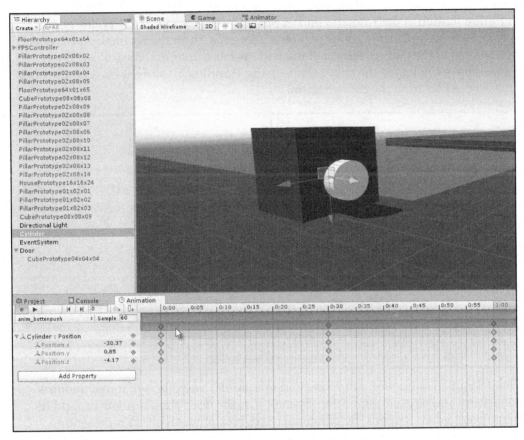

Creating a button push animation

The start and end key frames should be identical, representing the button in its neutral, or resting, position. The middle key frame, by contrast, represents the button as pushed inwards in its socket (the true push state). To create this key frame, simply drag the red time slider to the middle of the timeline in the **Animation** window, and then move the button into the position in the scene. This arrangement of key frames ensures that when the button push occurs, the button begins in a neutral state, then goes inwards, and finally returns to its neutral state. To enhance the smoothness of button motion at the start and end of the animation, you can flatten the curve handles using the Curves Editor, which is accessible from the **Animation** window, by clicking on the **Curves** button at the bottom-left corner of the window. If you cannot move or change the curve shape using **Handles**, then right-click on the point and choose **Flat** from the context menu.

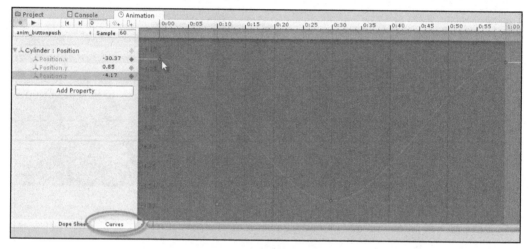

Smoothing button motion

The door-open animation can be created in a similar way, though it may require some extra stages of configuration. Specifically, the door should rotate around its hinge point when it opens. By default, a cube, box, or mesh object representing the door will not always have its hinge (pivot) at the correct position for creating a rotation animation. We would not, for example, want the door to rotate around its center. This can be fixed easily from within Unity, by simply parenting the door mesh to an empty object positioned at the pivot location, and then by animating the *parent instead of* the door mesh directly.

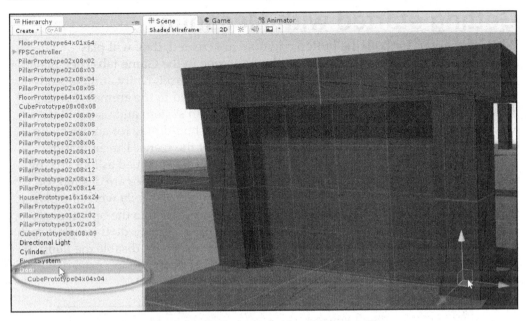

Creating a pivot point for the door-open animation

For the door-open animation, two key frames should be created: one at the beginning of the animation (closed) and one at the end (open). As with the button-push animation, the Curves Editor can be used to smooth the animation motion with ease-in and ease-out effects.

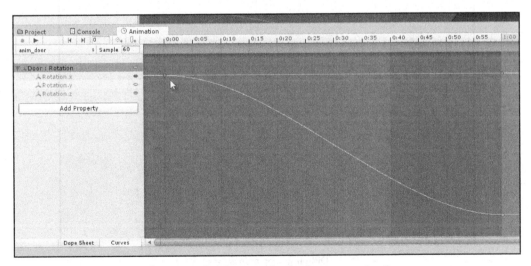

Defining an animation curve for the door-open animation

Getting started with Mecanim

When animations for both the button and door are created, they will play automatically in a loop every time you play the scene in the **Game** tab. They play automatically because upon creating an animation clip asset, Unity automatically generates an `Animator Controller` asset that is assigned to the animated object in the scene. The controller itself is part of the Mecanim system and uses a **State Machine** to define how and when an animation clip should play for an object. By default, it plays the animation clip at the beginning of the scene. The animations play on a loop because all new **Animation Clip** assets are specified as loopable by default. Neither the automatic playback nor the looping behavior are desired for the animation here, because the button animation should play *only* when the player presses the button, and the door should open *only* in response to the button push. Let's first disable the looping behavior of each animation clip. To do this, select each animation clip in the Project panel, and in the Object Inspector, disable the **Loop Time** checkbox. This prevents all animations from playing in a loop. Instead, they will play only once and then stop.

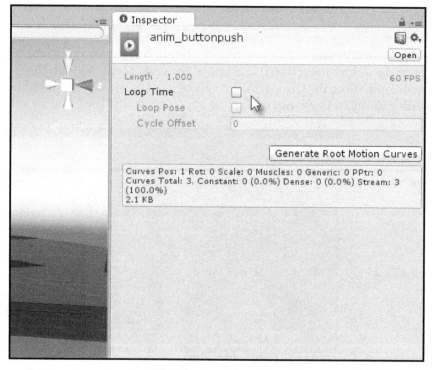

Disabling loop animations

Even if looping playback is disabled, the animations will still play automatically when the level begins, albeit once. This is because the **Animator Controller** asset is assigned to each object—the door and the button. To change this behavior, we'll need to open the Animator window. You can do this by going to **Window | Animator** from the application menu, or you can double-click on the **Animation Controller** asset from the Project panel. The controller assets are generated alongside the **Animation Clip** assets.

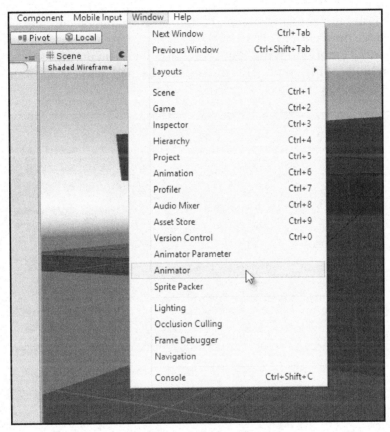

Accessing the Animator Controller

When you select the button object in the scene and view the Animator window, you'll see a Mecanim state machine, composed of connected nodes (called **states**). The states control how and when animation clips should play on the object at runtime. By default, the green **Entry** state is connected directly to the **anim_ ButtonPush** state (or whatever name you assigned to the button push animation). The **Entry** node fires, or is activated, when the scene begins. At this point, the execution (or logic) of the graph follows the connections wherever they lead. For this reason, the button-push animation plays automatically when the scene begins, because the **Entry** nodes connect to the button-push animation clip. Let's rewire this graph to behave differently. To start, right-click anywhere in the graph area, and go to **Create State | Empty** from the context menu. When you do this, Mecanim creates a new empty node in the graph. This means the attached object in the scene will *do nothing* when this node is active.

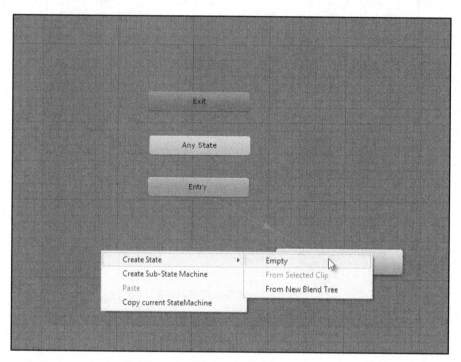

Creating an empty state in the Mecanim graph

However, the newly created node is connected to nothing. This means that it will never be active because there is no connection to it from the **Entry** node, which is where the graph always begins. The **Entry** node always connects to the default node, which is highlighted in orange. For now, select the newly created empty node and name it Idle by typing in the **Name** field in the Object Inspector.

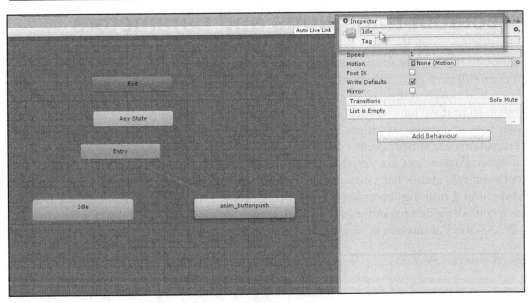

Naming Mecanim nodes

As mentioned, the **Entry** node always connects to the default node, which is orange. Let's make the **Idle** node default. To do this, right-click on the **Idle** node and select **Set as Layer Default State**. The **Entry** node now connects to the **Idle** node instead. This means that the button-push animation will no longer play automatically when the scene begins, which is what we wanted. Well, it's halfway to what we wanted!

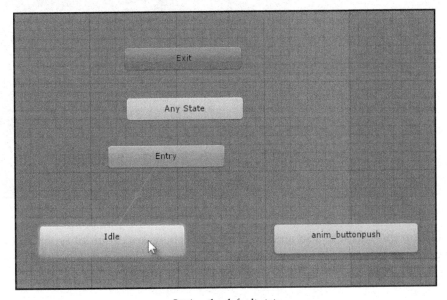

Setting the default state

Mecanim transitions and parameters

The problem with the push-button Mecanim graph created previously is that although it prevents any animation from playing automatically at scene startup, there's still no way to initiate the push-button animation when it's supposed to play later, that is, when the player clicks on it. The aim now is to rewire the Mecanim graph so that we have control over when the button-push animation plays, allowing playback at an arbitrary time. To achieve this we'll use **transitions** and **parameters**. Transitions are simply connections between states that allow one state to move to another. Parameters are variables, or switches, that we can create to fire a transition between two states. Let's now create a parameter that'll help us control when the **Idle** state (doing nothing) becomes a button-push state. Effectively, this parameter will act as a control switch for initiating animation playback. Inside the Animator window, click on the **Parameters** tab in the top-left corner.

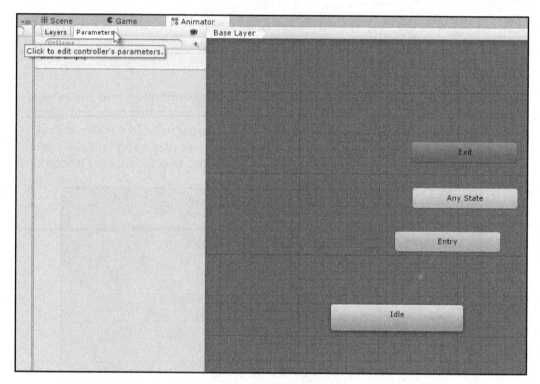

Accessing the Parameters tab

Then click on the + icon to add a new parameter. There are different types that can be selected. For this sample, select **Trigger**. Triggers act like control switches—once activated, they will fire a transition from one state to another.

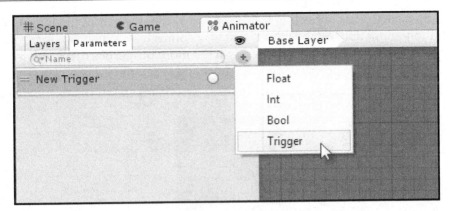

Creating a trigger

Assign the trigger a name, such as PushButton. Once created, the trigger appears in the parameter list and features a checkmark icon next to its name, which can be pushed at runtime for debugging and testing purposes, allowing us to activate the trigger directly from the editor. Now that the trigger has been created, it must be linked to a transition in the graph to be really effective. A transition should be created between the **Idle** state (doing nothing) and the push-button animation. This creates a link between the **Idle** state and the animation. To create the transition, right-click on the **Idle** state in the graph and then choose **Make Transition** from the context menu.

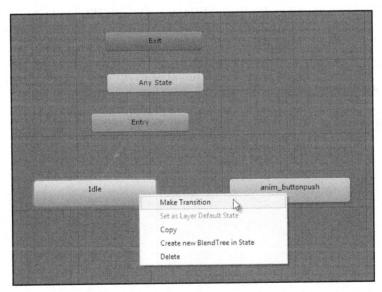

Creating a transition

You can then click on a connecting transition arrow that runs from the **Idle** state to the button-animation, establishing a one way connection. When you select the transition arrow between the states, you will see more properties displayed in the Object Inspector. These properties control how and when the transition occurs.

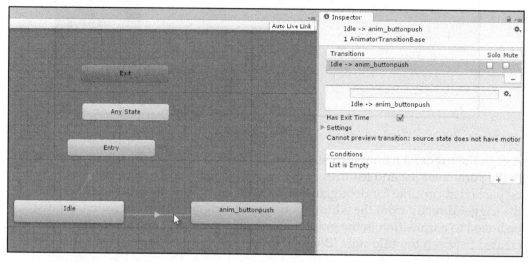

Selecting a transition displays more properties in the Object Inspector

By default, the transition occurs at exit time, which means that the **Idle** state plays once, or for a period of time, and then automatically transitions to the button push state, even if the player does not press the button. This can be confirmed by playing the scene and observing what happens to the button object in the **Scene** tab; it'll just push inwards automatically, a few seconds after the scene start. In contrast to the default settings, the transition should occur when the **PushButton** trigger is activated. To achieve this, disable the **Has Exit Time** checkbox from the Object Inspector when the transition is selected. This prevents the **Idle** state from automatically transitioning to the button-push animation.

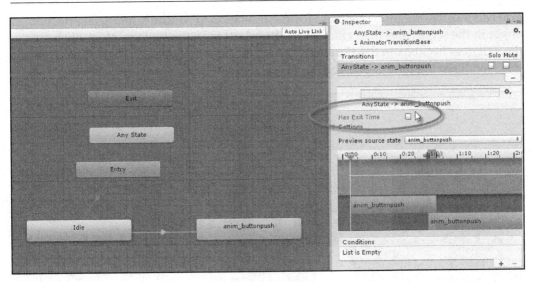

Disabling Has Exit Time

Next, the **Conditions** panel in the Object Inspector can be used to specify when the transition should be activated. Click on the **+** icon to add a new condition. Then, from the drop-down list, select the **PushButton** trigger, if it's not already selected. This finally connects the **PushButton** trigger to the transition.

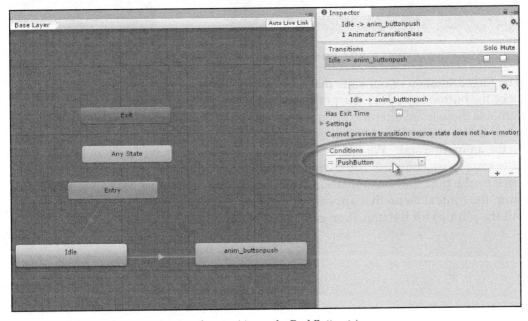

Connect the transition to the PushButton trigger

You can test the trigger connection for the transition at runtime. Just select the button object in the scene, and then click on the **Play** button in the toolbar. Next, click on the **Trigger** checkbox in the **Parameter** panel of the Animator window. When you do this, you'll see the button push animation activated in the **Scene** or **Game** tab.

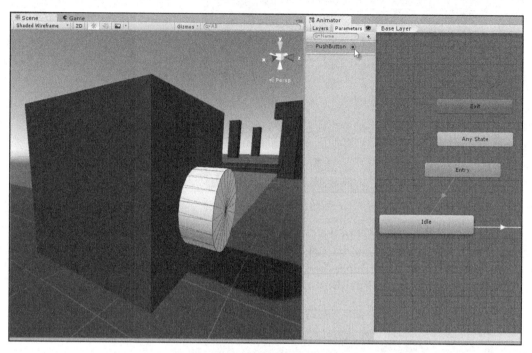

Testing the PushButton trigger

The final limitation of our state machine for the button in the Mecanim graph is that once the button is pushed, the graph transitions to the push-animation state and remains there, even after the animation completes. This means that the player cannot push the button a second, third, or fourth time simply because the graph "gets stuck" in the animation state. We want the button-push animation to transition back to the **Idle** state when completed, allowing multiple button pushes. To achieve this, right-click on the push-button animation state in the graph and select **Make Transition** from the context menu that appears. Then drag a connection back to the **Idle** state. All the settings for the transition can be left at their default values.

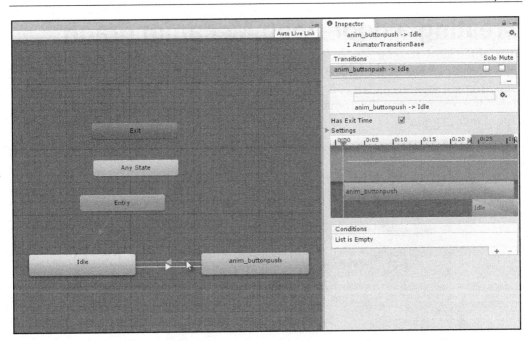

Creating a two-way connection between states

This now completes the Mecanim graph for the button object in the scene. As we've seen, the connectivity between the trigger and transition can be tested at runtime from the Animator window. But even so, the player *still cannot* trigger the transition by clicking on the button object in the scene. This will be fixed soon, after considering the use of the Mecanim graph for the door.

Creating a door-open Mecanim graph

Everything shown so far for creating a push-button animation can be repeated for a door-open animation, which may be launched using a trigger. Consider the following screenshot, with a complete Mecanim graph for a door. It features an **Idle** state (door closed), and this transitions to a door-open animation, activated by the **OpenDoor** trigger.

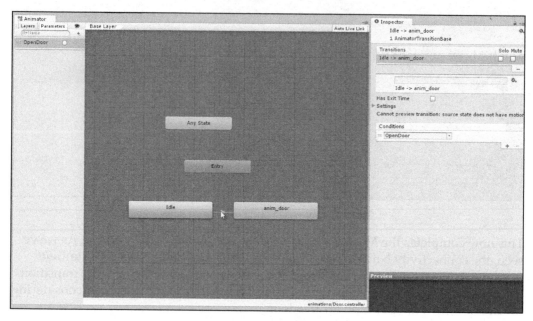

A complete Mecanim graph for the door

The door-open graph can be tested, much like the push-button graph. Just select the door object in the Scene or Hierarchy panel, play the game, and then click on the **Door Open** trigger in the **Parameters** panel of the Animator window. The door should open in response.

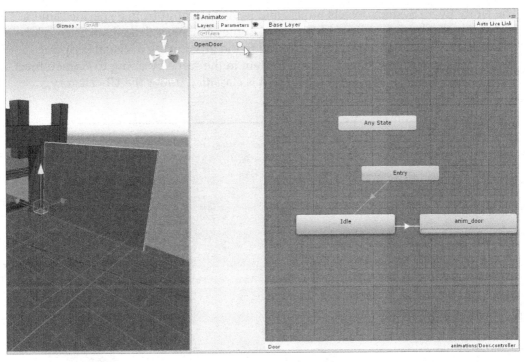

Testing the door-open animation

Creating scene interactions

The sample scene we're creating here finally has two animation clips (button-push and door-open), and two animation controllers that define how the clips relate to states in a scene object. In the previous sections, the controllers have been configured with triggers so that for both the door and the button, their animations can be played back on demand, simply by activating the respective trigger. Now, the problem is that the player cannot activate the triggers themselves *in the game*. Only we, as developers, can do that using the Unity editor during play mode. Our aim now is to have the player press the button to open the door. This means that a button push should activate both triggers in the animation controllers: one for playing the button animation, and the other for opening the door. There are many ways to achieve this interactivity. One way is through scripting, but we don't need to go that far. We can use the Unity Event System. In this section, we'll see how.

The Unity Event System detects mouse and keyboard input from a specific camera and automatically determines which object in the scene was clicked on. Then it lets us define the way to appropriately respond to the input using a Visual Scripting system. To get started, create an Event System in the scene by going to **GameObject | UI | Event System**. Although this option is classified under the **UI** category, it actually has many uses outside UIs.

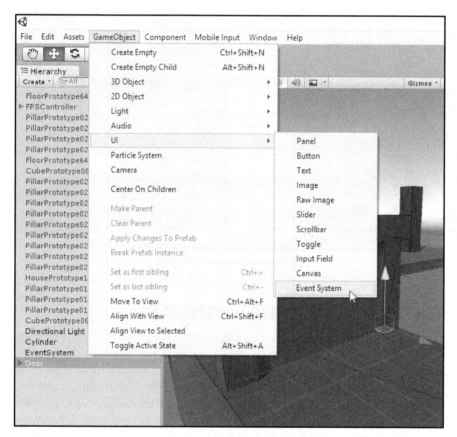

Creating an Event System

Next, find the main camera in the scene and select it. For the sample scene included in this book's companion files, the camera is attached to the FirstPersonCharacter. Once it is selected, add a **Physics Raycaster** component to the object by going to **Component | Event | Physics Raycaster** from the application menu. Adding this to the camera allows the Event System to detect on-screen clicks and determine which object in the scene was under the cursor at the time of the click, based on where the camera was focusing. It's important to attach this component to the game camera—the camera through which the player sees the world—or else clicks won't necessarily be detected for the appropriate objects.

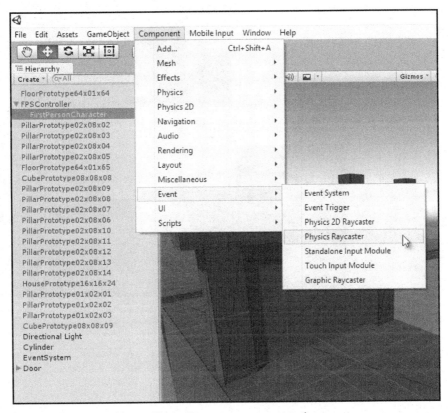

Adding a Physics Raycaster component to the camera

After adding an Event System to the scene and a **Physics Raycaster** component to the camera, we're ready to start configuring the button object to play the required animations. Select the button object in the scene (the object that should be clicked on by the player to open the door), and add an **Event Trigger** component by going to **Component | Event | Event Trigger** from the application menu.

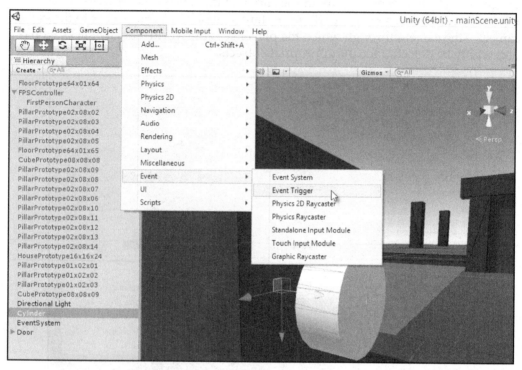

Adding an Event Trigger component to a button object in the scene

After adding an **Event Trigger** component to the button object, click on the **Add New Event Type** button from the Object Inspector. This indicates that we want to listen for a specific event and be notified when it happens. From the context menu that appears, select the **PointerClick** event.

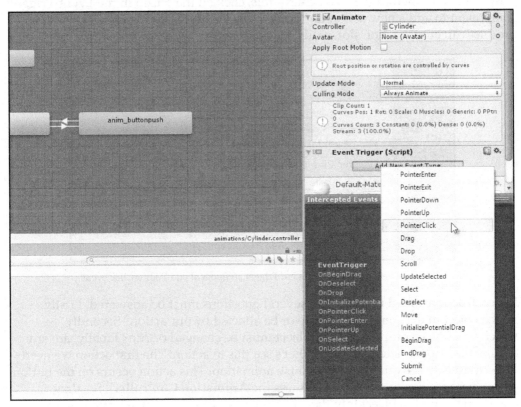

Handling a PointerClick event

This adds a new section, or panel, to the component from which we can choose a set of actions to perform when the **PointerClick** event occurs for the button. Specifically, two actions should be performed. First, we should activate the button animation using the trigger **PushButton**, and then we should activate the door-open animation using the **DoorOpen** trigger. To achieve this, click on the + icon in the **Event Trigger** component to add a new action underneath the **PointerClick** event category. This produces an empty action slot, ready to be defined.

Creating a new action for the Event Trigger component and PointerClick event

For each action added to the event, several questions must be answered. Firstly, which object in the scene will receive or be affected by our action? Secondly, which function or property of that object must be changed or run? Finally, are any arguments or parameters required? Let's see this in action. The first action we need to perform is to activate the button-push animation. This action occurs on the button object (because the button object features the **Animation Controller**). So, drag and drop the button object into the game object slot to specify the button as the target object.

Specifying a target object for an action

Next, for the function drop-down, go to **Animator Component | SetTrigger(String)**. This indicates that for the button object, Unity should activate a trigger when a click occurs.

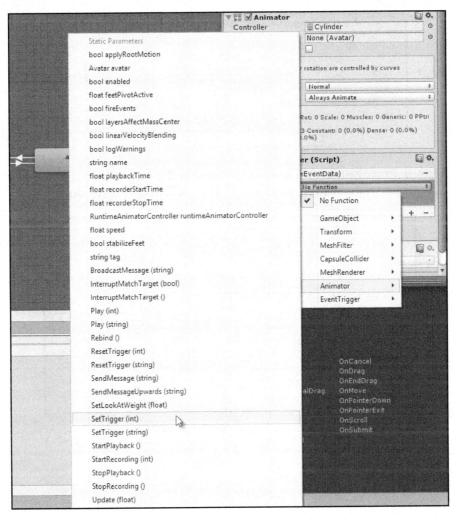

Setting a function for the button object action

Finally, in the string field, enter the name of the trigger that should be activated. For the button object, this should be **PushButton**, matching the name of the trigger defined in the Mecanim animation controller.

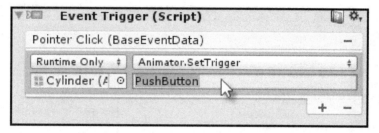

Setting a function for the button object action

Click on the **+** icon again to add a second action for the door object, using the **SetTrigger** function to set the **OpenDoor** trigger, which opens the door.

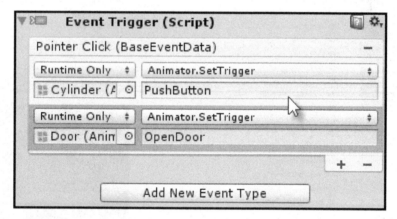

The completed Event Trigger component for the button object

Now we're ready to take the project on a test run, being able to open the door by clicking on the animated button. To test this successfully, make sure that the mouse arrow is over the button when clicked on, and both the button animation and door animation will play automatically. Splendid work! You have now configured an interactive, animated scene using Mecanim.

Opening the door using a button press

Summary

This chapter showed you how to create an interactive scene using animation clips, and covered the Mecanim system and the Event System. Using a combination of these three features, we created an animated scene in which pressing a button opens a door. Although simple in design and principle, this sample uses a wide range of animation features and demonstrates just how much can be achieved in terms of functionality using only animation and no scripting. In the next chapter, we'll get started with character animation in Mecanim.

5

Character Animation Fundamentals

This chapter marks the beginning of our analysis of character animation, which continues into the next chapter. In this chapter, we'll consider the issues of character importing and configuration, and the techniques and workflows required for getting the most from our characters during animation. Specifically, we'll look at mesh importing, avatars, skeletons, muscles, retargeting, and root motion. So let's go!

Creating rigged characters

For characters to animate properly in Unity, they must first be rigged inside 3D modeling software, such as 3ds Max, Maya, or Blender. **Rigged** means that an underlying skeleton or humanoid bone structure is added to the model by the artist, and each bone (such as the arm bone, leg bone, and so on) is specifically weighted (magnetized) to the vertices of the mesh. The purpose of the bones is to define the extent to which vertices in the character mesh should move and deform to conform to the skeleton.

This makes character animation easier because instead of animating a high-resolution character model and all its vertices, the animator can simply animate the skeleton (bones) and have the character deform automatically to match that skeleton.

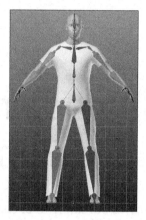

A rigged character

The full details of character rigging and the rigging process are software-specific and beyond the scope of this book. This book assumes you already have a rigged character to import. However, you can generate rigged characters quickly and freely using the MakeHuman software. This software can be downloaded from `http://www.makehuman.org/`. More information on generating rigged characters for Unity can be found online at `https://www.youtube.com/watch?v=IflzMxdvEtQ`.

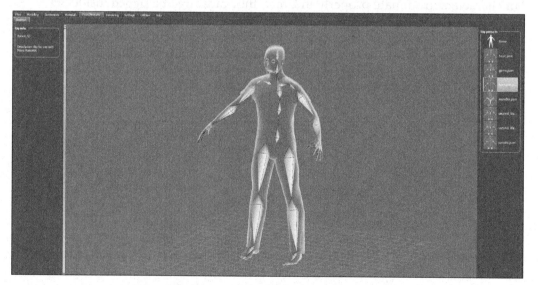

A rigged character created inside the MakeHuman software

The complete project for this section can be found in this book's companion files, and includes a rigged MakeHuman character. It is in the `Chapter05/char_anim_walk_end` folder.

You can also find premade rigged characters in the characters asset package in Unity 5. This package can be imported by going to **Assets | Import Package | Characters**.

Importing rigged characters

Importing rigged characters into Unity is initially a drag-and-drop operation. Just drag your FBX character from Windows Explorer (or Mac Finder) into the Project panel, and Unity will load both the mesh and its rig automatically. The mesh should be displayed in the Preview panel. However, as we'll see later, it's possible to import only a rig and animation data minus the mesh. For the purposes of demonstration here, we'll use the MakeHuman rigged character included as part of this book's companion files in the `Chapter05/Char_Anim` folder. This mesh is shown in the following screenshot.

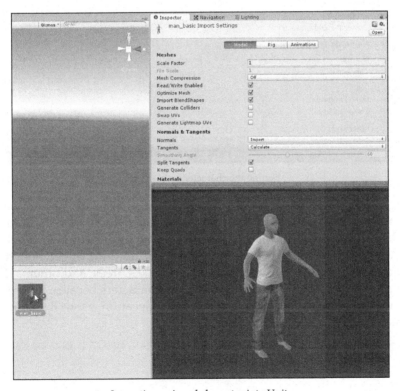

Importing a rigged character into Unity

The first step for importing a rigged character is deciding on **Scale Factor**, as changing a character's scale factor later can sometimes corrupt or invalidate other settings of the mesh. To do this, drag and drop your character mesh into a scene, checking out its proportions and sizes in relation to the rest of your scene. Ideally, *stick to real-world units*; that is, use the meter as a unit of measurement where one Unity unit corresponds to 1 meter. This means you should change your scale factor if required so that your mesh appears to be of a real-world size in the scene. This is important for both physics and lighting calculations.

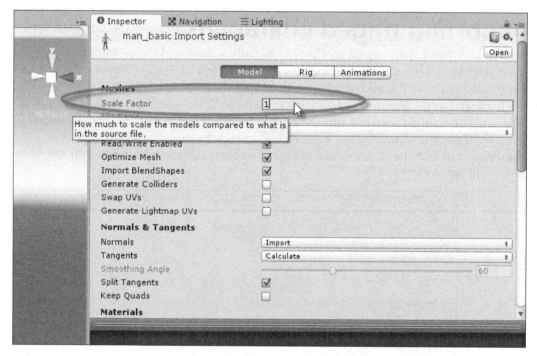

Setting the character's scale factor

Next, switch to the **Rig** tab in the Object Inspector, and from the **Animation Type** drop-down list, select **Humanoid**, if it's not already activated. By default, this value will probably be **Generic** if the mesh contains rigging information, or **None** if the mesh has no rigging information. **Generic** should be used for rigged noncharacter meshes, such as cranes, three-headed monsters, snakes, trees, and others. **Humanoid** is the recommended setting to choose for human characters because it gives us access to the entire range of animation features in Mecanim, as we'll see later. After **Humanoid** is selected, click on **Apply**.

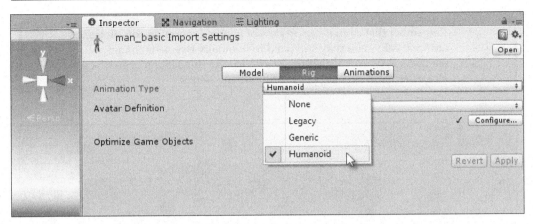

Selecting Humanoid from the Animation Type menu

When you click on **Apply** to confirm a **Humanoid** rig, a check-mark or a cross will appear beside the **Configure** button in the Object Inspector. This indicates whether or not Mecanim has successfully identified a humanoid character rig inside the mesh file. For the character mesh provided with the book, and for the sample asset meshes, Unity should successfully detect the character rig data. However, if your own meshes fail, they will need to be configured manually. We'll see how to do that next.

Avatars and retargeting

Selecting a **Humanoid** rig for an imported character mesh means that Unity will automatically try to configure your mesh in a special way that Mecanim requires. It does this using a data structure, called an **Avatar**. When the autoconfigure process completes, your mesh will either pass or fail the autoconfiguration process. If the process fails, then you will certainly need to configure your mesh Avatar manually. To do this, click on the **Configure** button to show the Avatar editor. Unity will switch to a different mode, and it may ask you to save your current scene before doing so.

Remember that even if the process of avatar generation completes automatically, you may still need to manually tweak or change a character Avatar. For that reason, don't skip this section even if your character mesh gets imported without any issues.

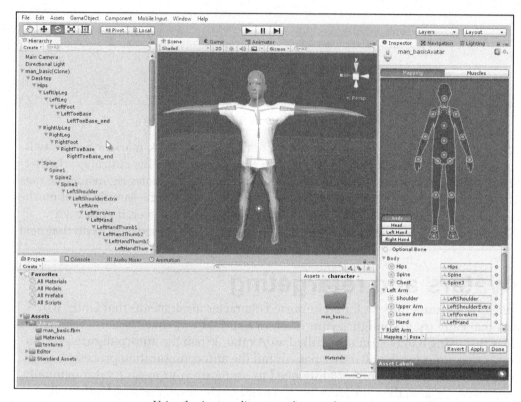

Using the Avatar editor to configure a character

The Avatar editor spans across three views in the interface, namely the Hierarchy panel, the Scene panel, and the Object Inspector panel (as shown in the preceding screenshot). Together, these constitute all of the data within the Avatar. The Hierarchy panel lists all the bones and their structure within the mesh. The Scene panel displays the character mesh alongside the bones. The Object Inspector panel, by default, displays a map of the human body. The idea of the Avatar editor is to ensure that all the appropriate bones in the mesh and hierarchy (such as the thighs, head, hands, shin, spine and so on) match the body map in the Object Inspector panel. Bones rendered in green inside the viewport are those that have been automatically and correctly mapped by Unity to the Avatar. Noncolored bones are those that have been ignored. Red bones are problematic; either their association to the map is wrong, or they are not oriented and aligned as they should be.

You can easily test and verify how the bones in the mesh have been assigned to the map by clicking on any of the circular icons on the body map. Doing this will select the corresponding bone object in the scene and hierarchy. By clicking on any of the circles, you should be able to verify that the correct bone has been mapped to the right location within the body map.

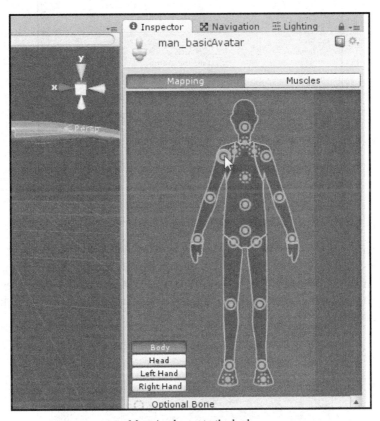

Mapping bones to the body

You can reassign any bone in the mesh to its correct place in the map by dragging and dropping the bone object from the hierarchy panel into the corresponding bone field in the Object Inspector.

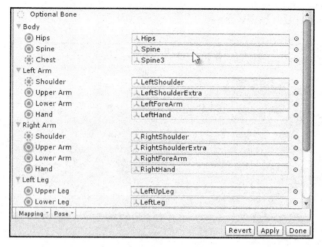

Remapping bones where required

Unless there are obvious red bones inside the viewport of the Avatar editor, it may not always be clear how the bones are related to the mesh and whether they will deform and animate as you expect. Therefore, you can perform a stress test on the mesh using the **Muscles** tab from the Object Inspector. To access this, click on the **Muscles** option.

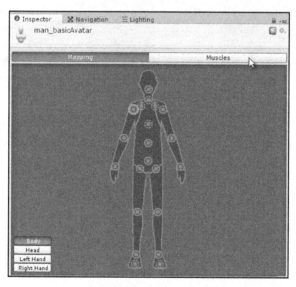

Accessing the Muscles tab to stress-test the mesh

When you access the **Muscles** tab, the character will enter a different pose in the viewport. Also, a new set of options will show up in the Object Inspector. Using the **Muscle Group Preview** sliders, you can push the character from neutral to extreme poses. This is useful because you can see how the character deforms in the skeleton across a spectrum of poses, allowing you to examine deformations at the extremes. This means that you can quickly identify any potential deformation issues.

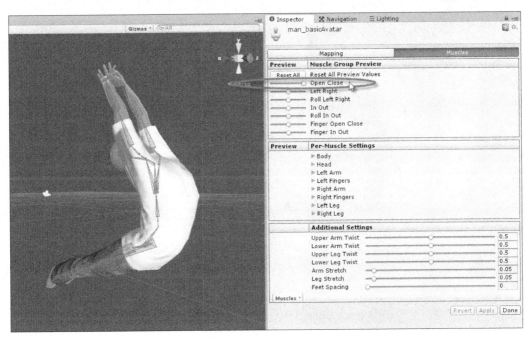

Push characters to extreme poses to test their deformation potential

If you're character isn't deforming properly in extreme poses, you can expand the **Per-Muscle Settings** group sliders to define the minimum and maximum extents for the deformations. In other words, the sliders control the limits to which the skeleton affects the mesh, allowing you to reduce or increase the deformation extremes.

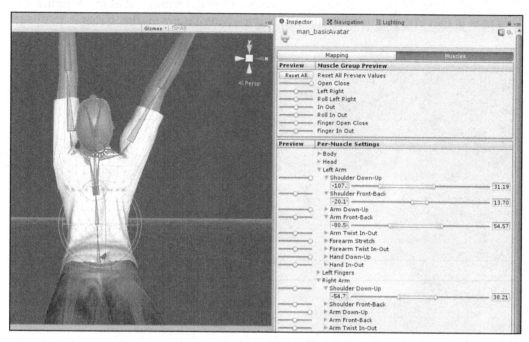

Correcting or adjusting extreme poses using the Muscles tab

When your avatar is working and deforming your character as needed, you can click on the **Apply** button. This configures the Avatar for the mesh file. A successfully configured Avatar is important for Mecanim because it lets you achieve retargeting. This means that *any* character with a correctly configured Avatar can be animated by the rig, and animations of *any* other character with a correctly configured Avatar. All rigs and animations are entirely interchangeable between all meshes with a configured humanoid Avatar, hence the name **Retargeting**—because the animation from one mesh can be retargeted to work on another. This lets you recycle and reuse all character animations. For example, you can make only one walk cycle and then share it for all walking characters.

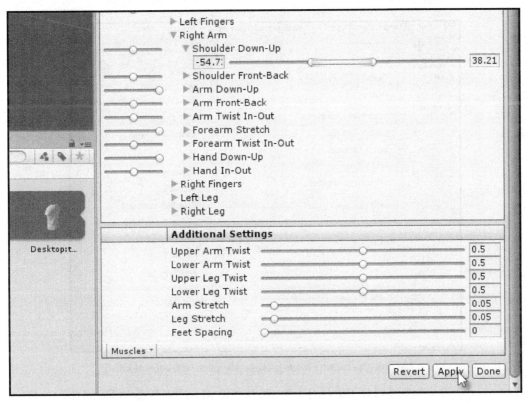

Click on Apply in the Avatar editor to create a working Avatar for a character mesh

Retargeting animations

The imported character included in this book's files features no animation data even though it's rigged. This isn't a problem, thanks to Avatars and retargeting. As mentioned, it's possible to take animations from a different character or file and apply it to any other character with a correctly configured Avatar. This section will demonstrate how such animation sharing works. To get started, import the characters asset package. This includes first- and third-person controllers alongside character animations for walk and run cycles. To get this package, go to **Assets** | **Import Package** | **Characters** from the application menu, as shown in this screenshot:

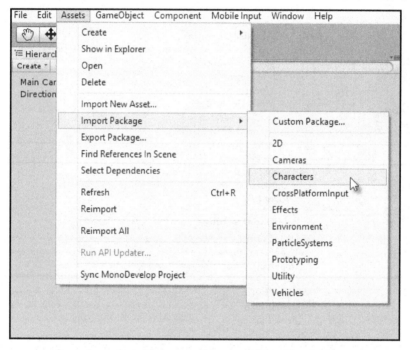

Importing a character assets package, complete with animations

The animations included in the package can be found in the Project Panel, by going to **Standard Assets** | **Characters** | **ThirdPersonCharacter** | **Animation**. The animations included there are FBX files, featuring rig and animation data but no mesh. To access the animation data, expand the mesh file and select the animation clip, as shown in the following screenshot:

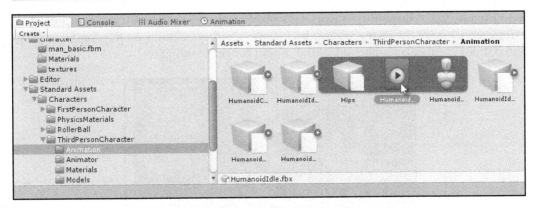

Selecting animation clips for retargeting

Most animations can be previewed in the Object Inspector using the default Unity model. By pressing **Play** on the toolbar, you can preview the character animation.

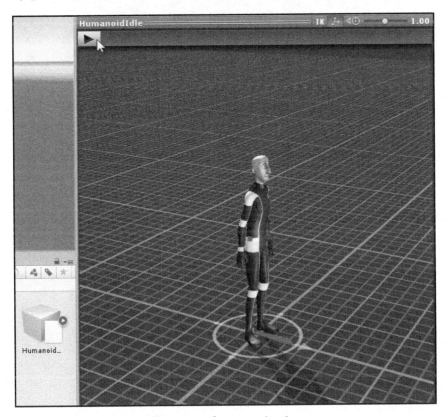

Previewing character animation

You can also see retargeting at work by sampling the animation for your imported character. Change the character model for previews by clicking on the Avatar icon in the bottom-right corner, and select the model for previewing.

Selecting an Avatar

After clicking on the Avatar, choose Other and then select your character model from the Project Panel. The preview panel will be updated in the Object Inspector to show the animation applied to the character. If everything looks good, then the Avatar is configured successfully for retargeting.

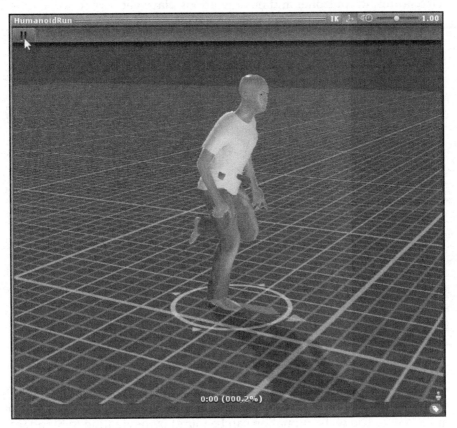

Retargeting in action

Let's give the model a quick try in a real scene, complete with an animation. To start, drag and drop the character mesh from the Project Panel to the scene, and position him at the world's origin, (0, 0, 0). Unity understands that the added character can accept animations in principle, so it automatically adds an **Animator** component, though it features no controller and no animations plays yet.

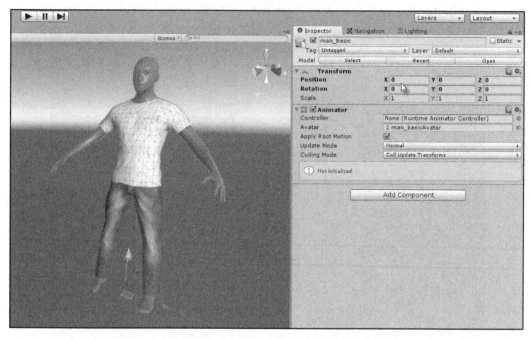

Positioning a character in the scene

Now we'll assign the character a walk animation. To do this, find the walk animation featured in the character assets package, and then drag and drop it onto the character mesh in the scene. The walk animation can be found by navigating to **Standard Assets | ThirdPersonCharacter | Animation**. The filename is `HumanoidWalk.fbx`. When you do this, Unity automatically configures an Animation Controller and assigns it to the **Animator** component.

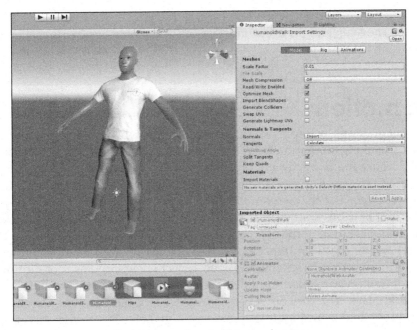

Assigning a walk animation to a character

Align your scene camera to get a good view of the character, and create a floor plane too. Then press **Play** on the toolbar. Immediately, the character will start walking. Congratulations! You've configured your first character for animation.

Creating a walking character

[The completed project at this stage can be found in this book's companion files in the Chapter05/char_anim_walk_start folder.]

Root motion

Based on the previous example, we've created a scene where an imported character undergoes a walking animation from the Unity characters package. On pressing Play, you'll notice the character not only *plays* a walk animation but actually *walks* forwards in the scene, as opposed to in-place walking. In other words, a walk animation plays *and* the character moves in terms of his scene position. This happens because of **root motion**. Root motion refers to any animation or change applied to the position and rotation of the topmost (root) object in the mesh hierarchy. The imported character mesh contains many child objects, for its bones and pieces. However, animation applied to the top-level object is regarded as root motion. By default, root motion is enabled for the character, which means that it will move when the animation plays. You can, however, disable root motion, causing the character to walk in-place, that is, walk without moving anywhere. To achieve this, select the character in the scene and disable the **Apply Root Motion** checkbox from the **Animator** component in the Object Inspector.

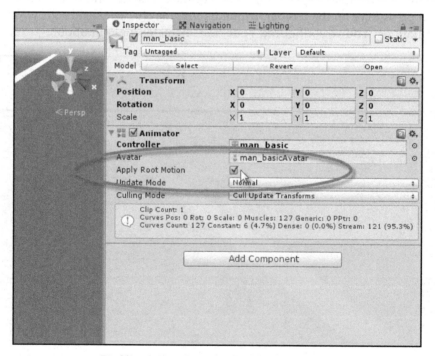

Disabling root motion animates characters in-place

Then, the question arises as to when root motion should be enabled or disabled. In short, root motion frequently makes character movement look more realistic, because with access to animation curve data, the motion of a character can be interpolated more effectively. However, disabling root motion gives you a faster and more responsive character motion, suitable for arcade and action games. Ultimately, the decision about when to use root motion depends on what's best for your game.

Fixing motion offsets

A common problem when importing root motion animations into Unity is related to offsetting. To see this problem, play the walking animation scene you've just created, or load it from this book's companion files in the Chapter05/char_anim_ walk_start folder. When you play this project and observe the character walking with root motion enabled, you'll see that not only does he walk forward in the scene, but he gradually wanders or moves off course. This is because he's not walking in a completely straight line. There's a degree of wander, or offset, that causes his path to deviate slowly over time. This isn't especially noticeable at first, but across larger spans of time, it's possible for a character to wander dramatically from its original path.

Root motion deviation

This problem is not scene- or character-related, but is embedded inside the animation root motion. To fix it, you should select the animation file in the Project Panel to display its properties. For the sample walk animation used here, the animation file can be found by going to **Standard Assets | ThirdPersonCharacter | Animation**. Select the `HumanoidWalk.fbx` file. In the Project Panel, select the **Animation** tab to view the animation data in the file. If you play the file in the Preview Panel, you'll see the offsetting problem there too.

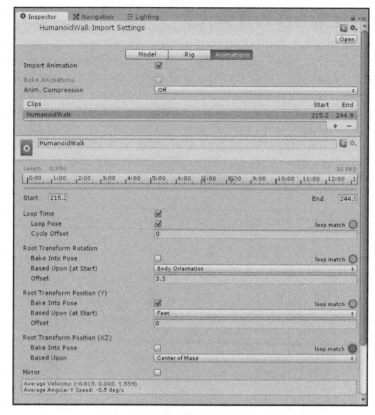

Viewing animation data for a selected file

The problem occurs due to the angular velocity. This value is shown in the Object Inspector. The **Average Velocity** vector indicates the direction and orientation of the character throughout the lifetime of the animation. For the default walk animation, this value includes a marginal, negative value for the x component of the velocity. Therefore, the model deviates from its course over time.

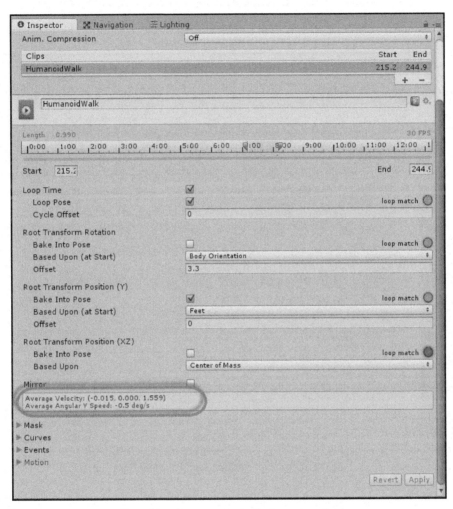

Examining the average velocity for root motion

To fix the issue, select the **Bake Into Pose** checkbox for **Root Transform Rotation** and change the **Offset** field until the **Average Velocity** value of the *x* parameter reaches **0**. The *z* value should remain nonzero, since the character should walk forward. To edit these settings, you may have to click on the **Edit** button in the top-right corner of the Object Inspector when the mesh is selected.

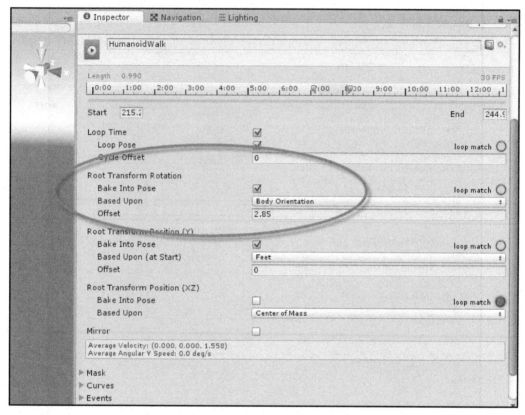

Adjusting root motion offsets with Bake Into Pose

Finally, if your characters appear to be walking through the floor, are centered on their hip bones, or are walking either higher or lower than they should be, you should change the **Root Transform Position (Y)** value to be **Feet**, for the **Based Upon (at Start)** field. This ensures that the root *y* position for your character is based on the feet bones.

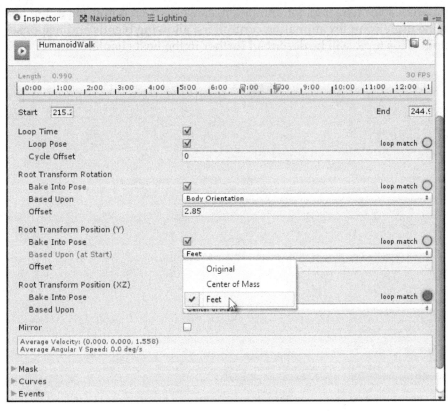

Setting the character's feet for animation

Summary

Congratulations! You now have a solid and versatile import workflow for adding rigged character meshes into Unity. They now play nicely with the Avatar system and can effectively reuse animations from many other suitable configured meshes. This, of course, is only half of the story. Mecanim not only allows you to import and configure reusable characters for animation, as we've been doing so far, but also lets you define more complex animation controllers, allowing blends and responses to user input. This topic will be described further in the next chapter.

6
Advanced Character Animation

In the previous chapter, we considered a "begin to end" workflow to import a rigged animated character model to Unity, configuring it to work optimally with the Mecanim system. By creating an Avatar for an imported character, we can make it work easily with a variety of different humanoid animations from many different sources. This is just one part of what makes Mecanim so powerful; but, there's more to Mecanim than this. After we've imported and configured a character, there are many features available for controlling and interacting with animations, making them work and play together to create believable characters at runtime. In this chapter, we'll consider these by creating a player-controlled character.

Creating a controllable character

This chapter explains how to create a player-controlled character with Mecanim from the ground up. The character will begin in an idle-neutral pose, and with the use of the WASD keys, the character will walk, run, and turn on the spot as appropriate. The project here will begin from a specifically prepared Start project, included in this book's companion files. This project contains only a blank scene, an imported MakeHuman character model, and the native assets for character animations, included in the character assets package. These animations include walk, run, idle, and turn animations (as discussed in the previous chapter). They were originally intended for a different character model, but the Unity Avatar system allows us to retarget different animations to multiple models, as we've seen before.

The Start project for this chapter can be found in the companion files inside the Chapter06/Start folder. The completed project can be found in the Chapter06/End folder.

Creating a player-controlled character with Mecanim

To get started with creating an animated character, ensure that you have imported humanoid animations for walk, idle, run, and turn (or use the animations included in the companion project). In addition, ensure that a character model has been imported and configured as an Avatar-compatible character, as explained in the previous chapter (or use the MakeHuman character model included in the companion project). Then create a new **Animation Controller** asset from the Project panel by right-clicking and going to **Create | Animator Controller**. The **Animation Controller** created will be used to control animations on the player rig when controlled using the keyboard.

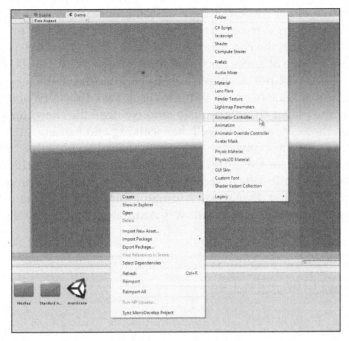

Creating an Animator Controller

Blend Trees

When we think about the playable character carefully, as shown in in the following screenshot, we can identify several states in which he can be in relation to the player input. Specifically, when the player is pressing nothing, the character should be in an idle-neutral pose, standing still and not moving at all.

A MakeHuman character to be animated

If the player presses either the left or right button only, the character should remain where he stands and turn in the appropriate direction. If the player presses the forward or up arrow key, the character should walk or run forward. Here, we can then identify a range of states for the character, such as idle, walk, run and turn. However, things are not as simple as this, because the character could turn *while* walking, or turn *while* running. In these cases, two directions of movement are provided by the player simultaneously, and we need the character to respond appropriately in these situations as well. For walking and turning, an animation should play, but it must also blend seamlessly and easily with animations from all other states to create the look and feel of an organic character. To achieve this, we can use Blend Trees, which allow us to smoothly blend multiple humanoid animations. To create a Blend Tree, first display the **Animator** window for the new **Animator Controller** asset. To do this, go to **Window | Animator** from the application menu, as shown here:

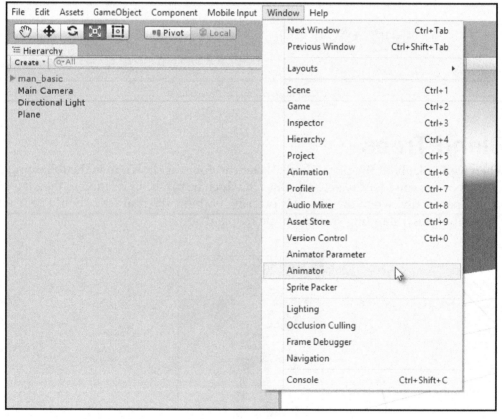

Show animator window

To create the Blend Tree, right-click inside the animator graph and go to **Create State | From New Blend Tree**, as shown in the following screenshot:

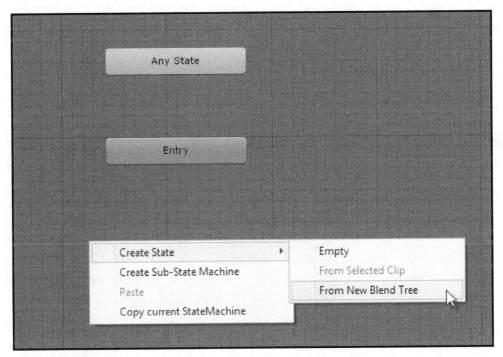

Creating a new Blend Tree

Once created, the Blend Tree appears as a regular animation node. If it's the first created node, then it'll appear in orange and be connected to the **Entry** node, since it automatically becomes the default node. If the Blend Tree node is not automatically connected like this, then right-click on the node and choose **Set as Layer Default State** to make the Blend Tree default. This means that the Blend Tree will automatically play when the game runs and the **Animator** is activated.

The Blend Tree, however, is a complex node compared to most animation nodes. It can be double-clicked on to reveal more options. By double-clicking on the Blend Tree in the graph, a new mode will be displayed in the Animator window, revealing more options. Using the Blend Tree interface, we can piece together a complex character animation. Notice that at the top of the Animator window, we can use the **Bread Crumb** trail to return to our previous view when we need to, simply by clicking on the **Base Layer** button.

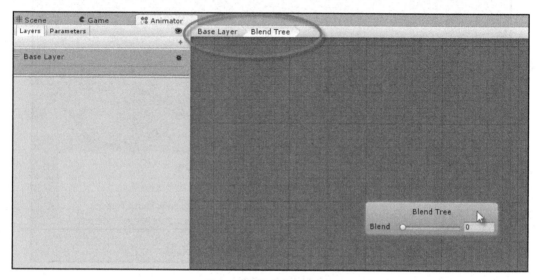

Using the Blend Tree mode

Dimensions

By default, every Blend Tree is configured to be one-dimensional. In other words, by default, every Blend Tree blends across a linear sequence of different animations. We can see this in the Object Inspector, as shown in the following screenshot:

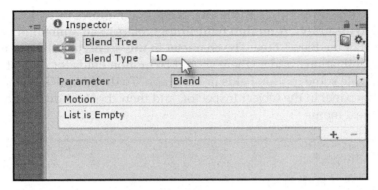

Setting the Blend Tree dimensions

One-dimensional Blend Trees may work well in a scenario where our character walks only forward and backward along a line, changing between idle, walk, and run states according to the player input. But in this case, our character should be able to turn, rotating to face new directions. Essentially, our character can move around on a 2D floor plane, and he responds to input from two axes (horizontal and vertical) instead of one. We should be able to use the up, down, left, and right keys to control the movement anywhere in the level. For this reason, change the Blend Tree type from **1D** to **2D Freeform Cartesian**.

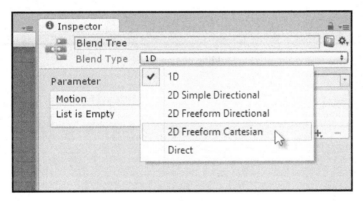

Using a 2D Blend Tree

When you create a 2D Blend Tree, the Object Inspector allows us to define motion fields to add to the graph. A **motion field** simply refers to an animation clip that should be part of the Blend Tree. The character in this scenario will have idle, walk, run and turn animations, and so there should be motion fields for each of these states. Let's create some motion fields in the graph. To do this, click on the **+** button in the **Motions** panel in the Object Inspector, and then choose **Add Motion Field** from the Context menu.

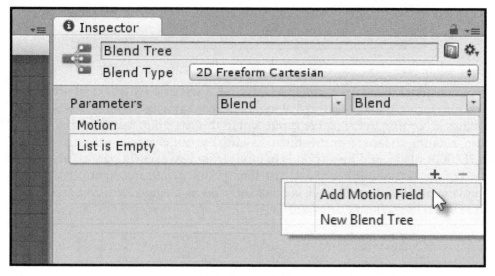

Adding motion fields

Click on the **+** button nine times to add nine motion fields. These will correspond to the following possible states for the character: idle, idle-turn-left, idle-turn-right, walk, walk-turn-left, walk-turn-right, run, run-turn-left, and run-turn-right. Each state requires us to use a slightly different animation clip, and we'll need the Blend Tree to blend them when the player provides an input. When you create two or more motion fields, a graphical representation of them appears in the Object Inspector.

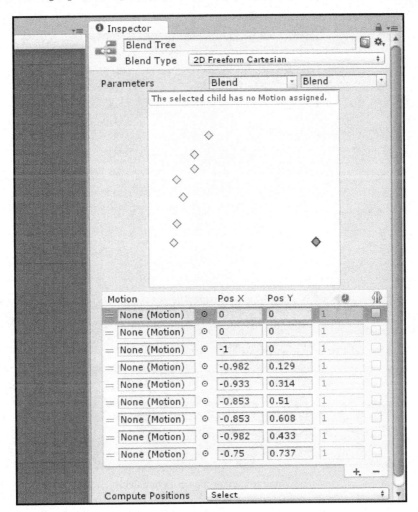

Visualizing motion fields

The added motion fields will likely create a scattered arrangement of nodes inside the graph, and this is not appropriate. We'll fix it in a moment. First, let's assign animation clips to the fields. To do this, go to the **Assets | Characters | ThirdPersonController | Animation** folder and assign clips to each appropriate slot. I've used the assignments shown in the following screenshot:

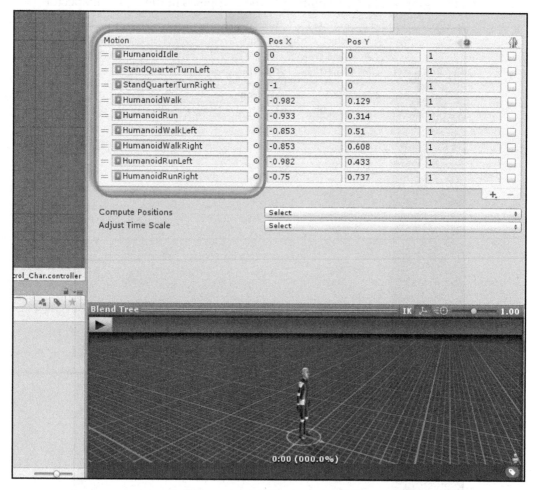

Assigning animation clips to motion fields

The animation clips have now been assigned to the relevant motion fields, but the fields themselves are inside the graph (as shown in the Object Inspector), and they still appear scattered, rather than systematically arranged in rows and columns. Let's fix this now by changing the **Pos X** and **Pos Y** values for each motion field. Doing this will arrange the motion fields to accept 2D input data appropriately. Consider this screenshot:

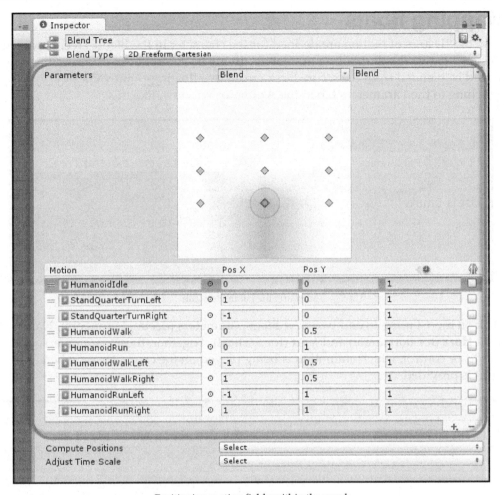

Positioning motion fields within the graph

Let's consider the arrangement of motion fields more carefully. The idle state is the neutral or resting pose, so this appears as the (0, 0) position in the graph. In contrast, running in a straight line is coded as (0, 1) and walking is coded as (0, 0.5), representing a state midway between resting and running. The turn states, by contrast, exist at the extremes of the *x* axis. Therefore, a running turn is represented by (-1, 1) (turning left) and (1, 1) (turning right).

Mapping floats

Now the 2D axes of motion are defined for the character in the Blend Tree. Next, we must create two floating-point parameters, giving us control over which animations should be blended from the script. First, create two floating-point values by switching to the **Parameters** tab in the **Animator** window, like this:

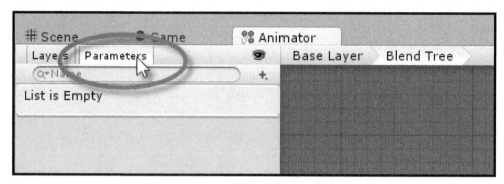

Accessing the Parameters Tab

Click on the **+** button to add two new **Float** parameters (decimal numbers). Name them **Horz** (for horizontal) and **Vert** (for vertical). Together, these parameters will decide, or control, which animation is being played on the character rig when an input is provided.

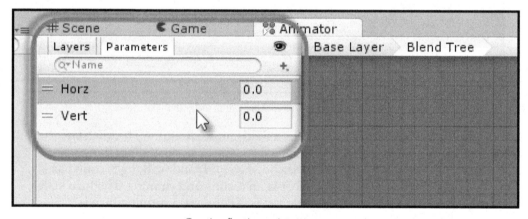

Creating floating-point parameters

Now that we've created two parameters, one for each axis of player input, let's map them to the Blend Tree in 2D Space. To do this, set the **Parameters** field in the Object Inspector. Click on the first (leftmost) drop-down list and assign it the value of **Horz** to map the **Horz** parameter to the *x* axis. Then repeat this procedure for **Vert**, mapping it to the *y* axis.

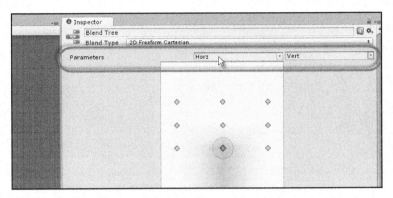

Mapping float parameters to the Blend Tree

When the mapping is established in this way, you can finally preview the animation and blend tree as a whole from the Preview panel in the Object Inspector. The Blend Tree node in the animator graph now features two sliders, representing your parameters. These allow you to scrub (slide) between the extremes, testing the blending combinations in the tree.

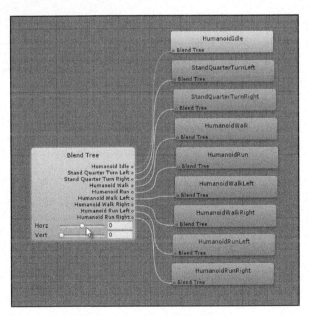

Testing the Blend Tree

To test the Blend Tree and verify that your motion fields are configured correctly, press the **Play** button on the tool bar in the Object Inspector. Then, adjust the slider fields in the Blend Tree to see the resultant animation. Your character motions should be looking good!

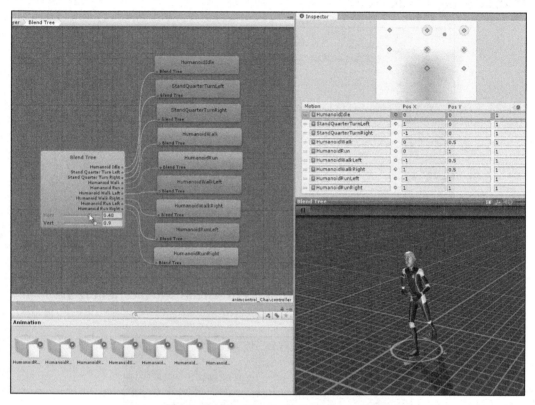

Playing the Blend Tree in the Preview panel

Preparing to script with Blend Tree animations

Throughout the previous sections, the Mecanim animator controller and its associated Blend Tree were fully configured to play a complete character animation. The different states (such as walk, run, idle, and so on) should not, however, be triggered arbitrarily. Instead, they should be triggered based on the player input through the WASD keys. To achieve this, we'll need to use a script, linking keyboard input to the Mecanim parameters. To get started, be sure that you've created a scene, you have a character, and you've assigned the **Animator Controller** asset to the **Controller** field of the object's **Animator** component. This ensures that the character model in the scene uses the appropriate Mecanim controller.

Assigning an Animator Controller to the character

Next, we'll need to create a C# script file that reads the player input and maps it to the controller parameters, playing the animation. To create a script, right-click inside the Project panel and go to **Create | C# Script** from the context menu, like this:

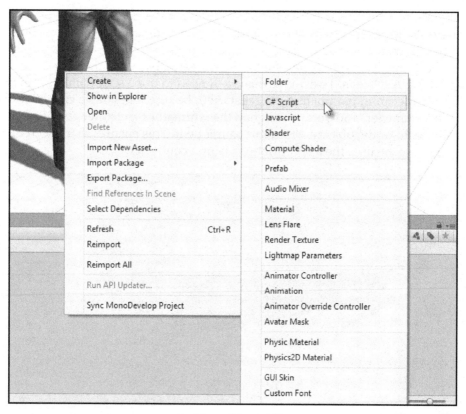

Creating a C# script file

Name the script file CharControl.cs. Then, drag and drop the file from the project panel onto the character in the scene, instantiating the script for the character.

Creating a CharControl script

Scripting with Mecanim Blend Trees

We're now almost ready to animate the player character from a script. We just need to define the newly created script file. Consider the following code sample, and then a deeper explanation will follow:

```
using UnityEngine;
using System.Collections;

public class CharControl : MonoBehaviour
{
  //Animator Controller
  private Animator ThisAnimator = null;
```

```
//Float names
private int HorzFloat = Animator.StringToHash("Horz");
private int VertFloat = Animator.StringToHash("Vert");

void Awake()
{
  //Get animator component on this object
  ThisAnimator = GetComponent<Animator>();
}

// Update is called once per frame
void Update ()
{
  //Read player input
  float Vert = Input.GetAxis("Vertical");
  float Horz = Input.GetAxis("Horizontal");


  //Set animator floating point values
  ThisAnimator.SetFloat(HorzFloat, Horz, 0.2f, Time.deltaTime);
  ThisAnimator.SetFloat(VertFloat, Vert, 0.2f, Time.deltaTime);
}
}
```

Here are some comments about this code:

- The `Animator.StringToHash` function is used to convert the parameter string names `Horz` and `Vert` into a more efficient integer variable that can be used later as an argument for the `SetFloat` function. By converting string names to integers for later use, we can make our code faster.

- Next, the `Animator.SetFloat` function is used to set the float parameters in the graph, controlling the animation.

Testing Mecanim Blend Trees

Let's test the code we created. Just press the **Play** button on the toolbar and hit the input keys to drive the character. If you select the character while the game is running and examine the animator window, you'll see the Blend Tree taking effect as you press the WASD keys to move the character. You'll see the transitions between different animations blend smoothly and seamlessly, appearing like one complete and self-contained animation sequence. Congratulations!

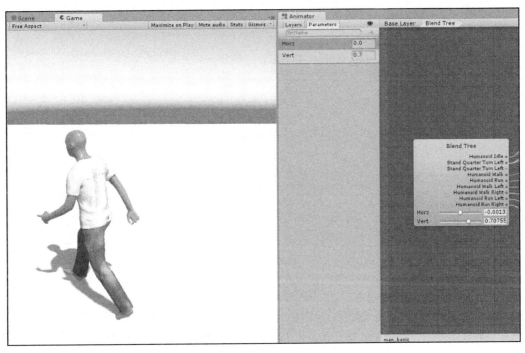

Testing the character animation

 The completed project can be found in the
Chapter06/End folder.

Summary

By this point, you should have a very solid foundation and understanding of
Mecanim, both for importing and configuring rigged characters, and for building
graphs and Blend Trees to support common animation needs that respond to player
input and controls. In the next chapter, we'll complete our tour of Unity animation
by covering blend shapes, animation curves, and movie textures.

7
Blend Shapes, IK, and Movie Textures

In this concluding chapter, we'll explore three largely unrelated animation methods available in Unity. These are Blend Shapes, for creating morph-like animations, such as lip-synch and facial motion; **Inverse Kinematics (IK)**, for posing character hands and feet at runtime; and movie textures, for playing prerendered movie files, such as MP4 files, on a 3D surface as a texture. All of these are less common animation methods in Unity, but can nonetheless play a powerful role in creating emotive and believable experiences. Let's consider each of them in turn.

Blend Shapes

If you need to create facial animation, such as facial expressions and lip synching, you'll often need to use Blend Shapes or morph animation. This kind of animation is usually created by an artist and animator in 3D software, and then it is imported into Unity. In terms of creation, it requires a two-step process. First, an animator defines all the possible and extreme poses of a face mesh; that is, they position and arrange all the vertices of a face mesh in their extremes, and create a Shape Key, or Blend Shape, to record the state of the mesh in that pose. By recording a series of different poses, the animator can then produce a facial animation in which an average expression is generated as a weighted blend between the ranges of different poses. Consider the next three screenshots, in which a monkey head mesh in Blender (http://www.blender.org) has been set to different and extreme poses. Each pose is recorded in a Shape Key, or Blend Shape. In the following screenshot we establish the initial or base pose. Sometimes called the resting pose..

The complete project for this section can be found in this book's companion files inside the `Chapter07/BlendShapes` folder.

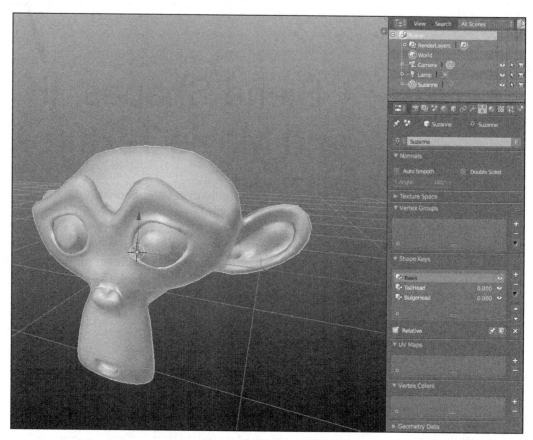

Basic pose for the monkey head

The following screenshot represents an intermediary pose:

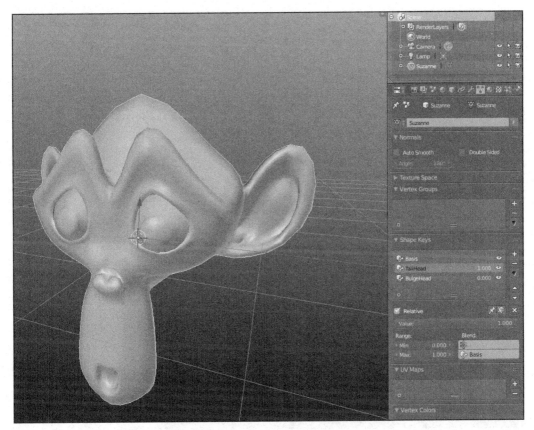

Extreme pose 1 for the monkey head

The following screenshot defines the final or looping pose:

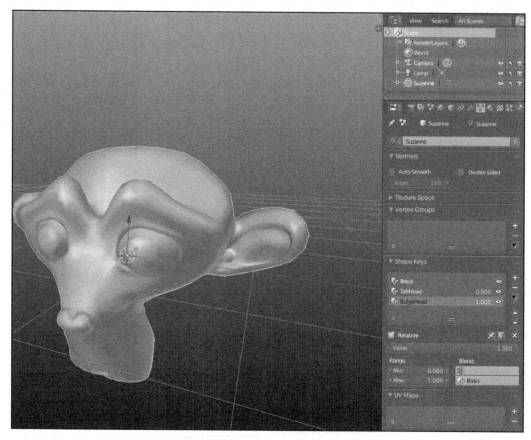

Extreme pose 2 for the monkey head

After creating a set of vertex arrangements and poses, you can export your mesh from the 3D modelling software via FBX format, as with regular meshes. The export steps differ from package to package. On importing the mesh into Unity, be sure to select the mesh in the Project panel and enable the **Import BlendShapes** option from the Object Inspector, as shown in the following screenshot:

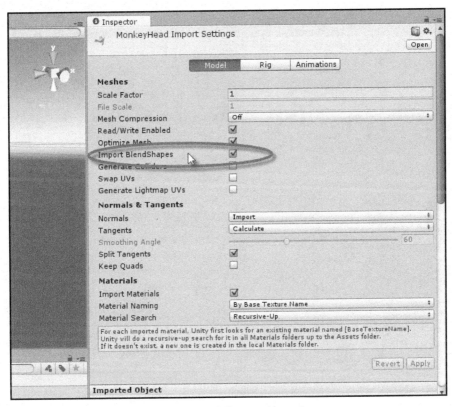

Importing Blend Shapes with meshes

You can easily test whether Blend Shapes have been imported properly for your mesh by dragging and dropping the mesh into the scene. Then, from the Object Inspector, expand the **BlendShapes** field. This field will list all the imported Blend Shapes.

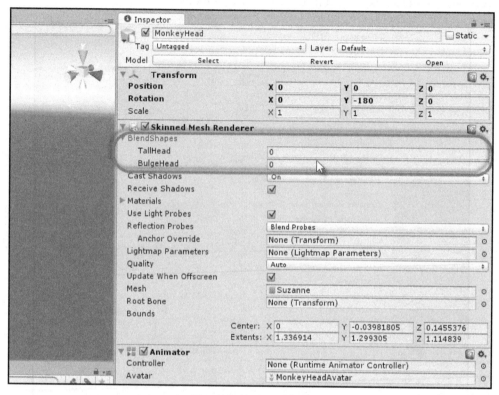

Accessing Blend Shapes for the selected mesh

Typically, the **BlendShapes** fields will map to your model within the 0-100 range. This means that a field will fully apply to your mesh when its value is 100.

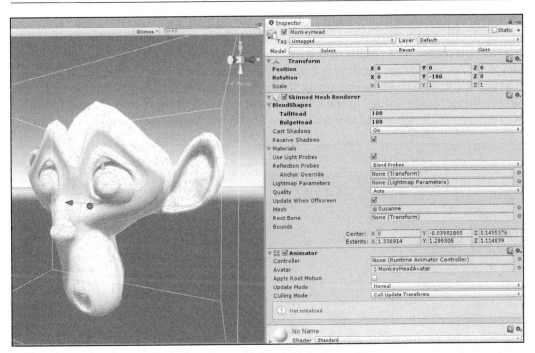

Testing Blend Shapes for the selected mesh

If you need to access or change the **BlendShape** weights and values from the script, you can use the `Mesh.BlendShapeCount` variable and the `SkinnedMeshRenderer.SetBlendShapeWeight` function (`http://docs.unity3d.com/ScriptReference/SkinnedMeshRenderer.SetBlendShapeWeight.html`).

However, you'll most likely want to animate **BlendShapes**. To do this, you can use the Unity **Animation** window by going to **Window | Animation** from the application menu. The details of this window were explained in the previous chapters. As with other mesh properties, you can record keyfames for Blend Shapes. Just scroll through the timeline using the mouse in the **Animation** window, and then set the **BlendShape** values in the Object Inspector for that time. In response, Unity will automatically generate key frames for the Blend Shapes over time.

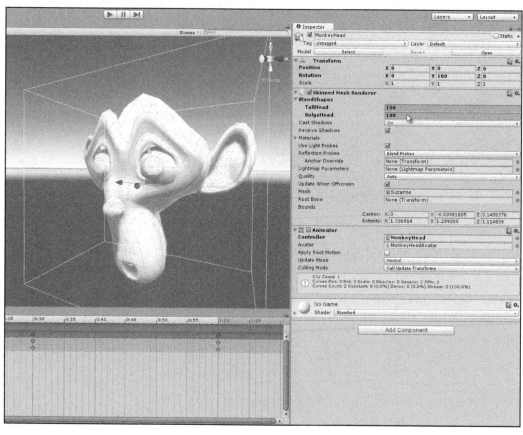

Animating Blend Shapes

Inverse Kinematics

Inverse kinematics is often shortened to IK, and it's highly important for achieving easy and believable character animation. Practically, IK lets you position hand or feet bones in a rig, and the remaining joints and bones will rotate and move automatically to achieve a believable look. In other words, for creating walk animations or pick-up animations, where a foot or hand comes in contact with a surface, IK saves the effort of animating all the bones involved, between either the foot and the hip, or the hand and the shoulder.

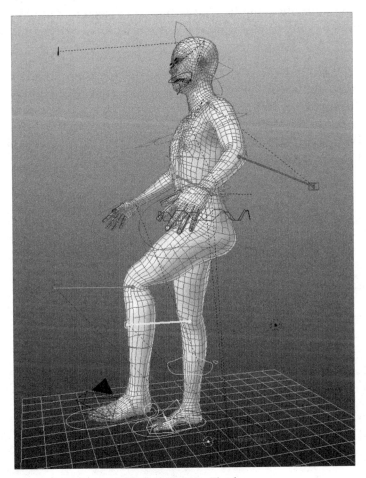

Configuring IK in Blender

Most 3D applications, such as Maya, 3ds Max, and Blender, provide options and features for creating IK. The purpose of these features is to help artists make animation simpler and easier. However, different programs store IK data differently, and this data is not typically transferable into Unity, even via FBX Files. This means that your character models will almost always be imported without IK data. This, however, doesn't mean that IK animations created in your 3D software will look any different when imported into Unity. It only means that all IK animations will be imported into Unity as **Forward Kinematics (FK)**. They will look identical, but will not give you any access to the IK features, not allowing you to easily pose and move your skeleton dynamically using IK. To fix this, you'll need to manually configure IK for your bones in Unity if you want access to IK features to dynamically pose the hands and feet of your characters.

To get IK to work properly, we first import a rigged character model into Unity. Then we select the model from the Project panel and enable the **Humanoid** rig, simply by switching to the **Rig** tab in the Object Inspector and selecting **Humanoid** for **Animation Type**. This does not enable IK per se, but configures your model to use the Mecanim Avatar system, which is required for IK. A suitable character model is included in the companion files in the Chapter07/IK folder.

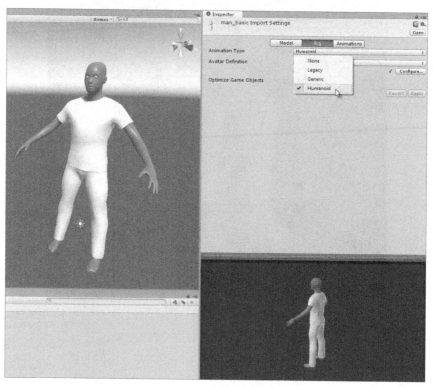

Configuring a character as a Humanoid rig

Let's now jump into using IK to control the character's hands, giving us independent control over hand placement and ensuring that all other arm bones will automatically bend and change to match the hand positions. To do this, create two new empty game objects in the scene. These will represent the control bones of the game character. These bones will be used to position the character's hands. Name the bones IK_LeftHand and IK_RightHand.

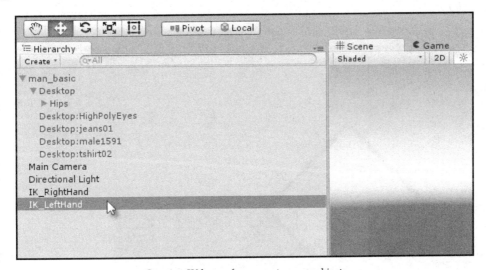

Creating IK bones from empty game objects

By default, the bones are not visible in the viewport unless selected in the Hierarchy panel. To make the bones into visible and clickable objects, select the cube tag icon in the Object Inspector and assign a 2D Gizmo representation to the object. Once selected, the bones can be both seen and selected from the viewport.

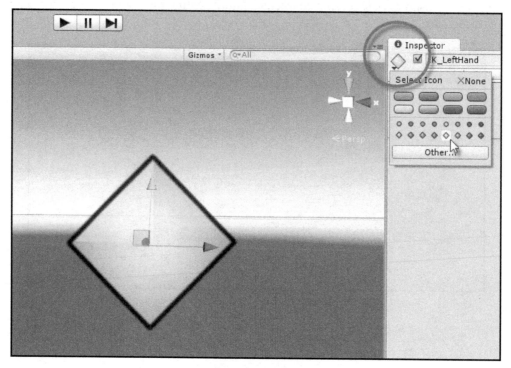

Making empties visible

Position each bone in the scene in front of the hand to be moved—the left bone in front of the left hand, and the right bone in front of the right hand.

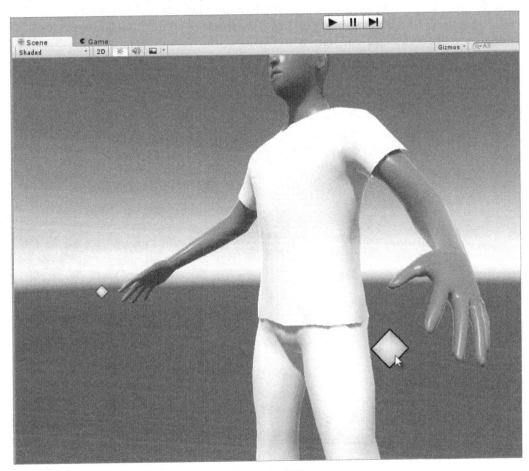

Positioning the IK bones

Create a new **Animator Controller** asset (animCharControl) and link the **Entry** node to an empty state. To create an empty state, simply right-click inside the graph and go to **Create State | Empty** from the context menu. Make sure that the empty state is the default node. Creating an **Animator Controller** asset is important for both animating a character and working with IK.

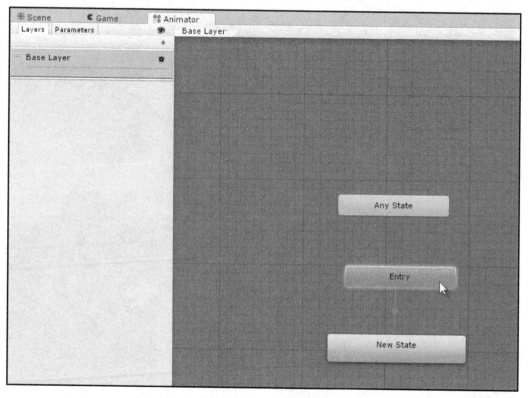

Creating a new Animator Controller asset

Make sure that the **Animator Controller** asset enables an **IK Pass**, allowing you to control the character IK programmatically in script. This is essential for using IK in Unity. To do this, click on the cog icon of **Base Layer** in the Animator window. Then select the **IK Pass** checkbox.

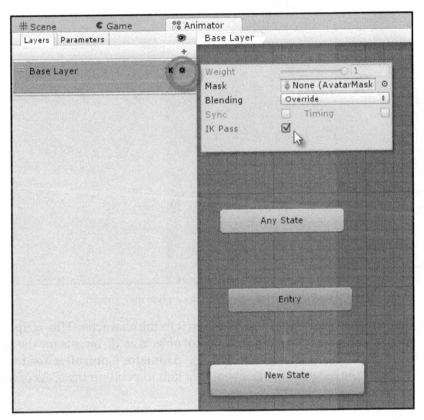

Enabling an IK Pass

Assign the controller to the character by dragging and dropping the **Animator Controller** asset from the Project panel onto the character mesh in the scene.

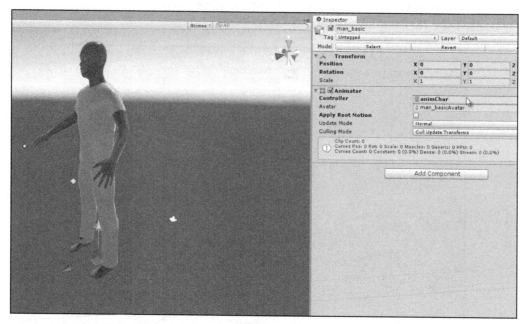

Assigning an Animator Controller asset to the character

Next, create the following script file and attach it to the character. This script file allows us to use the left- and right-hand control objects as IK targets for the arms. Because the **IK Pass** checkbox was selected, the **Animator Controller** asset will automatically call the OnAnimatorIK event function to position the arms of the skeleton on the specified objects:

```
using UnityEngine;
using System.Collections;

public class ArmIK : MonoBehaviour
{
  public float leftHandPositionWeight;
  public float leftHandRotationWeight;

  public float rightHandPositionWeight;
  public float rightHandRotationWeight;

  public Transform leftHandObj;
  public Transform rightHandObj;
  private Animator animator;

  void Start() {
```

```
        animator = GetComponent<Animator>();
    }
  void OnAnimatorIK(int layerIndex) {
     animator.SetIKPositionWeight(AvatarIKGoal.LeftHand,
leftHandPositionWeight);
     animator.SetIKRotationWeight(AvatarIKGoal.LeftHand,
leftHandRotationWeight);
     animator.SetIKPosition(AvatarIKGoal.LeftHand, leftHandObj.
position);
     animator.SetIKRotation(AvatarIKGoal.LeftHand, leftHandObj.
rotation);

     animator.SetIKPositionWeight(AvatarIKGoal.RightHand,
rightHandPositionWeight);
     animator.SetIKRotationWeight(AvatarIKGoal.RightHand,
rightHandRotationWeight);
     animator.SetIKPosition(AvatarIKGoal.RightHand, rightHandObj.
position);
     animator.SetIKRotation(AvatarIKGoal.RightHand, rightHandObj.
rotation);
    }
}
```

Attach the script file to the character. Then drag and drop the left- and right-hand objects into the appropriate `Transform` slots in the Object Inspector. Next, set the weightings to **100** to ensure that the bones will affect the object.

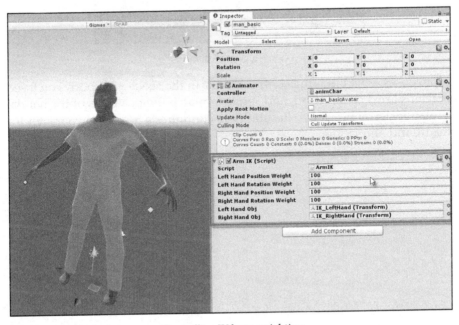

Controlling IK bone weighting

Now take the game for a test run and see IK in action. The character should begin in a default pose, but his arms will magnetize towards the control objects for the hands.

Testing the IK bones

For test purposes, when moving control objects in the scene viewport, you'll see the character's arms move, bend, and rotate to match the positions of the hands. Congratulations! You now have the ability to configure a Mecanim character for real-time IK and animation.

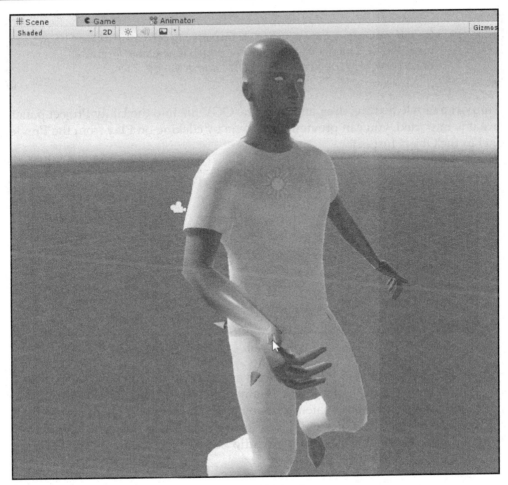

Positioning the hands

Movie textures

Textures are images that are displayed on a 3D geometry. Most textures are two-dimensional, static images, such as JPEG and PNG files. However, Unity also supports animated textures in the form of video or movie textures. These allow you to import movie files into your project and use them as textures. The movies can play with sound and be presented in-game. Therefore, they are especially useful for creating cut-scenes, credit sequences, flashbacks, advertisements, and other special effects. They are, however, resource heavy, making them a big hitter on performance. For this reason, you should use them sparingly. Unity supports different movie formats, but the recommended format is OGV (the Ogg Theora video). More information on this format can be found online at http://www.theora.org/.

Even if your movies are not in OGV format, you can easily convert them using the VLC media player software, which is available for free at http://www.videolan.org/vlc/index.en_GB.html.

To import a movie texture, drag and drop the OGV file into the Unity Project panel. Once it is imported, you can preview the movie by clicking on **Play** from the Preview panel in the Object Inspector.

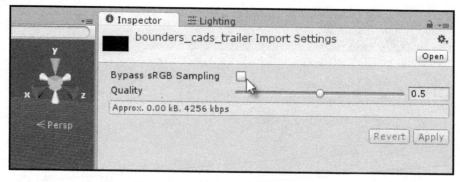

Importing movie textures from OGV files

Next, create a plane object in the scene to act as a surface on which the movie will play at runtime. To create a plane, go to **GameObject | 3D Object | Plane** from the application menu. Once it is created, add an **Audio Source** component to the object, which will be responsible for playing the movie audio. To do this, select the **Plane** object and go to **Component | Audio | Audio Source** from the application menu.

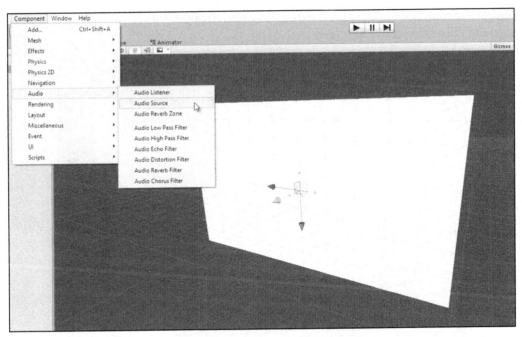

Creating a plane object to play movie files

Then create a new material to be applied to the mesh for showing the movie texture. To create a new material, right-click inside the Project panel and go to **Create | Material** from the context menu. For the shader type, navigate to **Unlit | Texture**. This will show the movie texture without being affected by the scene lighting.

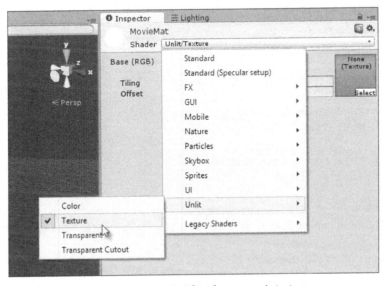

Create a texture material to show a movie texture

Assign the material to the plane by dragging and dropping it from the Project panel onto the **Plane** object in the scene.

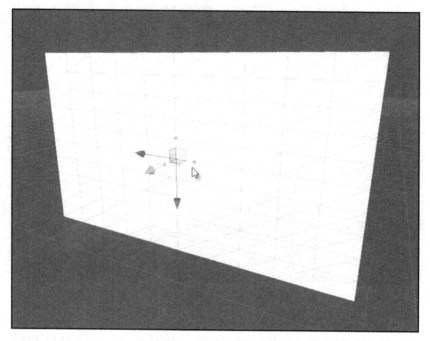

Assigning a material to the plane

Now create a new C# script file to play the movie texture and its associated audio. The following sample demonstrates the code required:

```csharp
using UnityEngine;
using System.Collections;

public class MoviePlay : MonoBehaviour
{
  //Reference to movie to play
  public MovieTexture Movie = null;

  // Use this for initialization
  void Start ()
  {
    //Get Mesh Renderer Component
    MeshRenderer MeshR = GetComponent<MeshRenderer>();

    //Assign movie texture
    MeshR.material.mainTexture = Movie;
```

```
    GetComponent<AudioSource>().clip = Movie.audioClip;
    GetComponent<AudioSource>().spatialBlend=0;

    Movie.Play();
    GetComponent<AudioSource>().Play();
    }
}
```

Drag and drop the script file onto the plane object in the scene, and then drag and drop the movie texture from the Project panel into the **Movie** slot on the **MoviePlay** component. This identifies the texture that should play for the material.

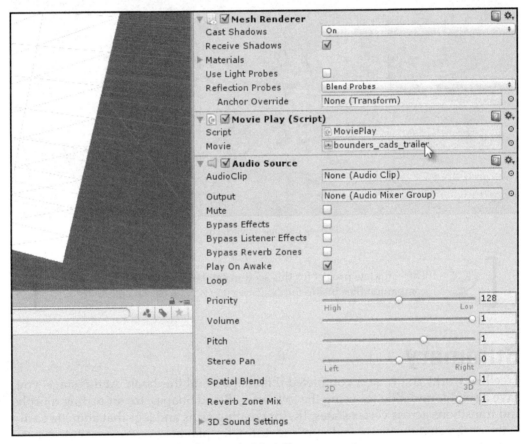

Configuring the MoviePlay component

Now click on **Play** in the toolbar to run the application. When you do this, the movie texture assigned to the plane will run automatically, complete with sound and music. Congratulations! You now have the ability to play cut-scenes, animations, and other prerendered sequences in your game.

Playing in-game movie textures

 The complete project for this section can be found in this book's companion files inside the `Chapter07/MovieTextures` folder.

Summary

Excellent work! You've now completed this chapter and this book. At this stage, you have a solid foundation for using the following: Blend Shapes, for animating morphs and transitions across vertex states; IK, for creating arms and legs that animate easily in the designated positions; and movie textures, for playing prerendered cut-scenes and other movie files.

Also, by completing this book, you've explored almost all of Unity's extensive animation feature set, including scripting and animation curves, animation windows, particle systems, rigged skeletons, key frames, interactive elements, and more.

Index

Symbol

3dmotive video course
  URL 13

A

animation
  about 1, 2
  creating, for button and door 82-85
  frames 2
  key frames 3
  retargeting 118-122
animation clip 49
animation curves
  about 20
  URL 20
  used, for coding tweens 20-23
  retargeting 118-122
animation, through code
  about 13-15
  animation, with coroutines 24-26
  camera shake effect 30-32
  consistent animation 16
  mapping animation 27-29
  material animation 27-29
  movement in direction 18, 19
  rotating, towards objects 24-26
  tweens, coding with animation
    curves 20-23
animation types
  about 3
  bone-based animation 5
  Morph animation 8
  particle animation 11

physics-based animation 7
programmatic animation 12
rigid body animation 4
sprite animation 6
video animation 9
Animation window
  about 49, 50
  accessing 51, 52
  animation channels, adding 55
  animation clip, creating 54
  animation play head, setting to preview
    animation frames 56
  docking, at bottom of interface 52, 53
  key frames, creating manually 58, 59
Avatar
  about 111
  retargeting 111-117

B

basic pose 151
Blender
  URL 151
Blend Shapes
  about 151-157
  using 151
Blend Tree
  about 133, 134
  animations, preparing to
    script with 145, 146
  creating 135
  dimensions 136-141
  floats, mapping 142-144
bone-based animation 5

physics-based animation 7
programmatic animation 12

R

retargeting 117
rigged 107
rigged characters
  creating 107, 108
  importing 109-111
  reference 108
rigid body animation 4
root motion 124, 125

S

scene
  preparing, with prototyping assets 79-82
scene interactions
  creating 97-105
Shuriken particle system 49
sprite animation
  about 6, 41, 42
  animation assets, setting 45, 46
  animation frames, correcting 46-48
  animation speed, changing 43, 44
sprite atlas 37-40
sprites
  about 34
  individual sprites 34-36
states 88

T

texture atlas 37
traditional flip-book animation 34
transform component 14
transitions 90
tweens
  coding, with animation curves 20-23

U

UI Canvas
  reference 63
Unity animation editor 49

V

video animation 9

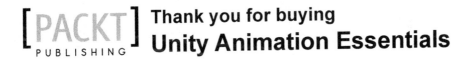
Thank you for buying
Unity Animation Essentials

About Packt Publishing

Packt, pronounced 'packed', published its first book, *Mastering phpMyAdmin for Effective MySQL Management*, in April 2004, and subsequently continued to specialize in publishing highly focused books on specific technologies and solutions.

Our books and publications share the experiences of your fellow IT professionals in adapting and customizing today's systems, applications, and frameworks. Our solution-based books give you the knowledge and power to customize the software and technologies you're using to get the job done. Packt books are more specific and less general than the IT books you have seen in the past. Our unique business model allows us to bring you more focused information, giving you more of what you need to know, and less of what you don't.

Packt is a modern yet unique publishing company that focuses on producing quality, cutting-edge books for communities of developers, administrators, and newbies alike. For more information, please visit our website at www.packtpub.com.

Writing for Packt

We welcome all inquiries from people who are interested in authoring. Book proposals should be sent to author@packtpub.com. If your book idea is still at an early stage and you would like to discuss it first before writing a formal book proposal, then please contact us; one of our commissioning editors will get in touch with you.

We're not just looking for published authors; if you have strong technical skills but no writing experience, our experienced editors can help you develop a writing career, or simply get some additional reward for your expertise.

Learning Unity Android Game Development

ISBN: 978-1-78439-469-1   Paperback: 338 pages

Learn to create stunning Android games using Unity

1. Leverage the new features of Unity 5 for the Android mobile market with hands-on projects and real-world examples.

2. Create comprehensive and robust games using various customizations and additions available in Unity such as camera, lighting, and sound effects.

3. Precise instructions to use Unity to create an Android-based mobile game

Unity 3D UI Essentials

ISBN: 978-1-78355-361-7   Paperback: 280 pages

Leverage the power of the new and improved UI system for Unity to enhance your games and apps

1. Discover how to build efficient UI layouts coping with multiple resolutions and screen sizes.

2. In-depth overview of all the new UI features that give you creative freedom to drive your game development to new heights.

3. Walk through many different examples of UI layout from simple 2D overlays to in-game 3D implementations.

Please check **www.PacktPub.com** for information on our titles

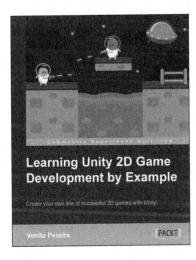

Learning Unity 2D Game Development by Example

ISBN: 978-1-78355-904-6   Paperback: 266 pages

Create your own line of successful 2D games with Unity!

1. Dive into 2D game development with no previous experience.

2. Learn how to use the new Unity 2D toolset.

3. Create and deploy your very own 2D game with confidence.

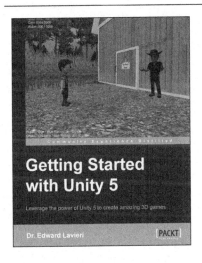

Getting Started with Unity 5

ISBN: 978-1-78439-831-6   Paperback: 184 pages

Leverage the power of Unity 5 to create amazing 3D games

1. Learn to create interactive games with the Unity 5 game engine.

2. Explore advanced features of Unity 5 to help make your games more appealing and successful.

3. A step-by-step guide giving you the perfect start to developing games with Unity 5.

Please check **www.PacktPub.com** for information on our titles

CPSIA information can be obtained
at www.ICGtesting.com
Printed in the USA
FSOW04n1515070416
18934FS